The Unbearable Light(ness) of AI

Weight and Lightness of Artificial Intelligence in Contemporary Society

Edited by Giuliano Pozza

OpenBook Publishers

https://www.openbookpublishers.com

Digital material and resources associated with this volume are available at https://doi.org/10.11647/OBP.0530#resources

Information about any revised edition of this work will be provided at https://doi.org/10.11647/OBP.0530

Open Reports Series vol. 15 | ISSN Print: 2399-6668 | ISSN Digital: 2399-6676

ISBN Paperback: 978-1-80511-898-5
ISBN Hardback: 978-1-80511-899-2
ISBN Digital (PDF): 978-1-80511-900-5
ISBN HTML: 978-1-80511-902-9
ISBN Digital ebook (epub): 978-1-80511-901-2
DOI: 10.11647/OBP.0530

Cover photos: Javardh, https://unsplash.com/it/foto/fotografia-afuoco-superficiale-di-piume-bianche-che-cadono-nella-mano-della-persona-FL6rma2jePU (front); Denis Poltoradnev, https://unsplash.com/photos/brown-and-white-concretebuilding-during-daytime-Jq1zrutUFP4 (back). Design by Jeevanjot Kaur Nagpal.

AUTHORS' AI DISCLAIMER: we believe that nowadays it is of paramount importance to be completely transparent about the use of AI in any human artifact. It is even more important in a book discussing AI and, among other topics, ethics in the use of AI. For this reason, at the end of every chapter there will be a specific AI disclaimer. Since we are a heterogeneous team of authors and we value diversity, you will discover that every author had a different approach in using AI to support her/his work. We believe this is another interesting peculiarity of our journey.

THE UNBEARABLE LIGHT(NESS) OF AI

Table of Contents

List of Illustrations

Figures

Tables

Foreword

Evelien Renders[1]

We live in an age where time no longer seems like a scarce resource. With AI at our fingertips, we can produce text, slides, images, videos and analyses faster than ever before. There is such allure in brainstorming while sipping our coffee, asking for deep research while doing something else, and receiving fluent answers instantly. These systems are tireless, polite, and always available, and their ease of use can make progress feel frictionless.

However, anyone who works seriously with AI knows that the allure of efficiency is in fact a restructuring of our time. We double-check outputs, question assumptions, and learn which tools we rely on for which tasks. We keep some on a short leash and give others more room, depending on context, risk and experience. We already relate to AI much like we relate to human colleagues: none are perfect, none are trusted blindly, but collaboration becomes effective once strengths,

1 President of EUNIS. EUNIS was formed in 1993 as the European University Information Systems association and registered as a non-profit organisation in Paris, France in 1998. The EUNIS community brings together those who are responsible for the management, development and the policy for Information Technology in Higher Education in Europe. The objective of EUNIS is to contribute to the development of high quality information systems. To achieve this, the aims of EUNIS are:

- encourage exchange, cooperation and debates between those responsible for information systems in higher education or research institutes/organisations within Europe;
- establish relationships with supervisory organisations in charge of information systems in higher education and in research institutes in each country as well as at European level.

Our mission is to help member institutions develop their IT landscape by sharing experiences and working together.

 https://doi.org/10.11647/OBP.0530.13

limitations and responsibilities are clear.

What academic research increasingly calls 'calibrated trust' and 'appropriate reliance' is therefore not an abstract concept, but a daily professional practice. It is about knowing when to use AI for exploration, structure or acceleration, and when human judgment, accountability and values must take the lead. These decisions are rarely technical alone; they are organisational, ethical and cultural. That is where community becomes essential.

For more than thirty years, EUNIS has brought together professionals working on digital transformation in higher education and research across Europe and beyond. Across many waves of technological change, the decisive questions were never only about what technology could do, but about how it reshaped institutions, governance, and professional roles. EUNIS exists to create space for shared learning across institutional and national boundaries, grounded in public values and responsibility.

Much of this work takes shape in EUNIS Special Interest Groups. These SIGs are not discussion forums, but working spaces where practitioners compare practices, test assumptions and develop shared language around complex topics. This book emerged from that ecosystem. It reflects how the community works: through dialogue, disagreement, and collective sense-making rather than isolated expertise.

EUNIS believes this book matters because it approaches AI in that same way. Instead of treating AI as a standalone technology, it explores its entanglement with sustainability, inclusion, governance and ethics, across world, organisational and personal levels. It shows how decisions made in one context shape consequences in another, and how responsibility cannot be neatly contained.

The chapters in this volume are grounded in practice and shaped through collaboration. They are the result of an intensive collective effort, carefully edited and coordinated by Giuliano Pozza, whose intellectual leadership and persistence made this book possible. The work was further supported by the EUNIS board and team, whose ongoing role in facilitating the community and enabling collaboration is indispensable. Without that shared infrastructure, a project like this could not exist.

In a world where AI can generate unlimited text, authorship gains weight rather than losing it. We read differently when we know who is speaking. Ideas land more deeply when they come from people whose experience we recognise and whose reasoning we can question. Books still matter because they offer sustained reflection, responsibility for ideas, and space for complexity.

This book does not offer simple answers. It offers a shared journey of inquiry into how we live and work with AI, and how we choose to exercise judgment in times of acceleration. What follows is an invitation to step into that conversation.

AI DISCLAIMER: the author used AI to support the final polishing of the foreword.

Preface

Giuliano Pozza

> It's a dangerous business, Frodo, going out of your door... you step onto the road, and if you don't keep your feet, there's no knowing where you might be swept off to.[1]

Writing this book, with so many wonderful contributors, has been an astonishing adventure indeed. We were literally not able to keep our feet from moving in so many different directions. We started from a general intuition, but we understood only along the way where we were heading: it was a marvellous surprise that we are enthusiastic to share with you. And, if you are reading so far, you are hopefully somehow intrigued by an intuition similar to ours or you are just curious about the title of this book (more on it in the Prologue!). But you are probably also wondering: 'With so many books about AI, do we really need one more?'

Of course, our short answer is yes. AI is indeed an inflated topic, in the same way as 'sustainability' and 'inclusion' are sometimes buzzwords. But the novelty of this book is that we are dealing with these three subjects together, exploring the relationships among them. And exploring these relationships at different levels.

Firstly, we will start studying AI, sustainability and inclusion at a global/general level, specifically speaking about sovereignty, sustainability and cybersecurity. The second level is the level of organisations/society. At this level we will discuss governance of AI in complex organisations, AI in medicine, AI in higher education and AI and the future of work. The third and final level is the personal/

1 J. R. R. Tolkien, *The Lord of the Rings: The Fellowship of the Ring* (Boston, MA: Houghton Mifflin Harcourt, 2012), p. 60.

 https://doi.org/10.11647/OBP.0530.14

ethical one. At this level, we will scrutinise the same topics focusing on ethics/equality, inclusion and accessibility and on the impact of AI on our minds. Some experts talk about macro, meso and micro levels. Of course, the three levels are intertwined, but not in a strictly hierarchical way. What impacts the personal level is changing society, and even the world. The global or organisational level topics have a direct impact on our lives as well. Because the reality is complex and borders are blurring. And AI is penetrating all levels of our lives.

Now that you have an idea of what you will find in this book, it is time to clarify who we expect 'you' to be. We are not writing this book for IT or AI experts. Yes, you need at least a general idea about AI (there are many introductory books that you can refer to), but who does not have it after November 30, 2022?[2] We are writing for anyone who is curious to understand what is below the surface of AI hype and explore the connections among the many buzzwords we mentioned above. If you still think you are in the right place, enjoy your reading and let us know your feedback. And please forgive us for the heterogeneity of the styles and tone of voices, since the authors come from different backgrounds: some are scholars, other professionals, all dedicated and enthusiastic. We tried our best to avoid being too academic, but we do believe diversity is a value, and it is indeed one of the characteristics of this book we do not want to give up.

And going back to adventures, I want to give a very special thanks to the companions of this journey, our 'fellowship of the book'. It has been really an incredible experience working with all the authors of this book and I am grateful for so much commitment and passion during the last months. We went out of the door and we stepped onto the road together almost one year ago. From that first step... so many virtual meetings, exchange of ideas, e-mails, peer review sessions, last minute calls, open discussions! And thanks to EUNIS and its President Evelien Renders for their enthusiasm and constant encouragement! I cannot forget the amazing EUNIS staff as well, in particular Jessica Schwarz for editorial and publishing support and all the others for helping us with the many activities related to writing and publishing a book.

I cannot end without another citation from the same source I used

2 The date when the first version of ChatGPT was made available to the general public.

at the beginning, which has been a lighthouse for all my life. Reading the next chapters, you will probably end up thinking that we do live in complex times. True, we cannot deny it. Complex and sometimes scary, but also interesting and full of opportunities. However, it is not up to us to choose our times. 'All we have to decide is what to do with the time that is given to us'.[3] We do hope that now, with the time that is given to you, you will decide to read this book and that it will prove a wise decision.

AI DISCLAIMER: the author did not use AI in writing the preface.

Reference

Tolkien, J. R. R., *The Lord of the Rings: The Fellowship of the Ring* (Boston, MA: Houghton Mifflin Harcourt, 2012).

3 Tolkien, *The Lord of the Rings*, p. 48.

Prologue

Giuliano Pozza

> The heavier the burden, the closer our lives come to the earth, the more real and truthful they become. Conversely, the absolute absence of burden causes man to be lighter than air, to soar into heights, take leave of the earth and his earthly being, and become only half real, his movements as free as they are insignificant. What then shall we choose? Weight or lightness? [...] When we want to give expression to a dramatic situation in our lives, we tend to use metaphors of heaviness. We say that something has become a great burden to us. We either bear the burden or fail and go down with it, we struggle with it, win or lose.[1]

'What then shall we choose? Weight or lightness?' This simple question, stated at the beginning of Milan Kundera's masterpiece *The Unbearable Lightness of Being*, is one of the reasons why we decided to call this book *The Unbearable Light(ness) of AI*. Because AI, as many other aspects of our lives, is a double-faced coin: on one side the light, or the lightness. To visualise this side, one need only think of all those who have used the first version of ChatGPT since November 30, 2022. Sam Altman, CEO of OpenAI, announced recently that ChatGPT hit 800 million weekly active users.[2] No one can deny that AI is a fundamentally disruptive technology. Sceptical as we were, after so many AI winters, those periods of collapsed funding that followed the broken promises of the 1970s and again in the late 1980s and 1990s, we have discovered a light and even a lightness, once we started playing with these tools ourselves. Who did not spend some time chatting idly with a bot or generating amazing

1 Milan Kundera, 'The Unbearable Lightness of Being', *The New Yorker* (1984).

2 Rebecca Bellan, 'Sam Altman Says ChatGPT Has Hit 800M Weekly Active Users', *TechCrunch*, 6 October 2025, https://techcrunch.com/2025/10/06/sam-altman-says-chatgpt-has-hit-800m-weekly-active-users/

 https://doi.org/10.11647/OBP.0530.00

images and videos with multi-modal AI tools? And who did not marvel at discovering what AI can do for medicine, for higher education or for professional and personal life at large in the last three years? You will find out more in the chapters of this book, but likely you already have more than one example in mind.

After the first exhilarating months, someone started wondering if all this AI circus could be sustainable in the long term. We started studying its social, economic and ecological impacts. We discovered that AI could be not only used but also abused. And that it could be abusive as well. We studied how the misuse of AI could impact negatively on cognitive processes, we faced new threats in cybersecurity with AI-powered attacks. Simply put, we discovered the dark side of AI.

For many of us, the lightness was gone and we learned how unbearable this light(ness) could be. This is the heavy side of the coin.

And here we need to go back to Kundera's question: lightness or weight, what is better? What should we choose? But is it really true that lightness is good and weight is bad? Because synonyms of weight are 'load' and 'burden', but also 'importance' and 'significance'. And the etymology of weight is linked to the idea of moving, pulling, driving.

We are starting to see different patterns in the use of AI. Some are quite worrisome, like the way a great number of students are using AI to boost their performance, missing the opportunity to improve their potential and their knowledge. A few patterns are definitely dystopian, like the manipulation of reality that some AI tools embed, which is even worse than the unwanted biases coded into all AI tools. But 'positive deviants' are emerging as well.

To clarify the concept, we need to go back to the observations of Jerry and Monique Sterning in rural Vietnam in the 1970s, where they found that in those same communities plagued with malnutrition, some families were able to raise their children in perfect health.[3] The first hypothesis was that these exceptions could be explained with the fact that they had access to additional resources: more personal wealth or a rich extended family. But it was not so. They were living with exactly the same resources of the other families, but were able to use them more

3 Jerry Sternin and Monique Sternin, *The Power of Positive Deviance: How Unlikely Innovators Solve the World's Toughest Problems* (Boston, MA: Harvard Business Press, 2010), p. xx.

efficiently and more intelligently: they were splitting the daily food in five meals or more, not only three. They were forcing the kids to finish their meal even if they were sick. They added simple but protein-rich additions to their food, like small shrimps or crabs. They consistently applied the habit of washing hands before meals. As a result, their kids' health was vastly improved.

AI is no different. Many of us have access to the same resources, but while some are able to empower themselves and to develop their full potential with the use of AI, others are using AI to cheat life. In medicine, for example, some physicians use AI as a shortcut, but a new generation of professionals is emerging, who are using AI as a superpower. With their wisdom empowered by AI, they give better diagnoses and identify the best therapies worldwide, leveraging an immense amount of scientific knowledge, nowadays impossible to master for a 'simple' human mind. This is a clear example of 'positive deviants' who can change the world.

Putting together lightness and weight is what the 'positive deviants' are doing, and it is the only way to comprehend and govern AI. We must not be blind believers, nor neo-Luddite sceptics. Probably we need to go back to Plato's attitude towards technology, which can be summarised in the posture of the 'sceptical believer' in the etymological sense.[4] In his famous argument against writing, which was the disruptive technology of his time, Plato, referring to Socrates' thoughts on writing, stated[5] (or paradoxically wrote):

> [writing] will implant forgetfulness in their souls; they will cease to exercise memory because they rely on that which is written, calling things to remembrance no longer from within themselves, but by means of external marks. What you have discovered is a recipe not for memory, but for reminder. And it is no true wisdom that you offer your disciples, but only the semblance of wisdom, for by telling them of many things without teaching them you will make them seem to know much while for the most part they know nothing. And as men are filled not with wisdom but with the conceit of wisdom they will be a burden to their fellows.[6]

4 Sceptical is from ancient Greek and its deep meaning is: compare, consider, inquire. Believer is coming from Proto-Germanic and it means to allow, to grant permission. So we should be inquisitive with new technology, but at the same time we should allow ourselves to get the best from what the technology can give us.

5 Using the words of Socrates.

6 Plato, *Phaedrus*, trans. Alexander Nehamas and Paul Woodruff (Indianapolis, IN: Hackett), 274c–275b.

A sceptic indeed, but also an innovator, able to overcome the position of his mentor Socrates and to massively use writing technology to document and communicate his ideas. Someone who allowed technology to enter his life, using it to transform the spread of knowledge but continuously questioning it: a sceptical believer. He was able to reconcile the light(ness) and the weight, not choosing one over the other, but embracing both. And this is probably the only truly human way to govern a technology as powerful as AI, avoiding intellectual enslavement to our own technology.

AI DISCLAIMER: the author did not use AI in writing the prologue.

References

Bellan, Rebecca, 'Sam Altman Says ChatGPT Has Hit 800M Weekly Active Users', *TechCrunch*, 6 October 2025, https://techcrunch.com/2025/10/06/sam-altman-says-chatgpt-has-hit-800m-weekly-active-users/

Kundera, Milan, 'The Unbearable Lightness of Being', *The New Yorker* (1984).

Plato, *Phaedrus*, trans. Alexander Nehamas and Paul Woodruff (Indianapolis, IN: Hackett).

Sternin, Jerry, and Monique Sternin, *The Power of Positive Deviance: How Unlikely Innovators Solve the World's Toughest Problems* (Boston, MA: Harvard Business Press, 2010).

1. Sovereignty and AI: The Weight We Choose

John Magnus Furseth Kallevik

> The struggle of man against power is the struggle of memory against forgetting.[1]

In 1997, Russian grand chess master Garry Kasparov met the supercomputer Deep Blue and learned that brute computing force could topple a chess grandmaster. Two decades later, South Korean professional Go player Lee Sedol faced the AI programme AlphaGo and saw a different evolution: a machine that played moves no human had imagined. Each match was a line crossed. Proof that AI keeps changing the rules while we are still teaching ourselves the game. Sovereignty in the context of AI means deciding what we let these systems teach us and what we refuse to hand over.

Here, sovereignty is not about flags or borders. It is the practical ability to steer your own digital fate: to know where your data lives, who can compel it, how decisions about you are made, and whether you can challenge them. It is the weight we choose to put on systems so they serve people, not the other way around.

The first encounters the average person had with modern artificial intelligence felt ground-breaking. For most people, it arrived quietly, like waking up one morning and discovering a new continent had appeared in the ocean overnight. You stepped onto this strange land with nothing but a keyboard and curiosity, and suddenly you were

1 Milan Kundera, *The Book of Laughter and Forgetting*, trans. by Michael Henry Heim (New York: Alfred A. Knopf, 1980), Part I (approx. pp. 12–46).

 https://doi.org/10.11647/OBP.0530.01

speaking to something that answered back. Not like a search engine, but like a presence. Fluid, adaptable, and startlingly confident, even when it should not be.

You asked it to write a letter. It did. You asked it to summarise an entire field of research. It obliged. You typed the vaguest description of a melody, and it somehow found it for you. Even composed a new one for you.

Released into the wild for us to test. And boy, did we test it. It tested us right back. Every prompt we typed was also a data point. Every correction we gave, every conversation we had, became training material. We were not just users exploring a tool; we were, knowingly or not, shaping what it would become.

It was intoxicating. The technology felt light, in the way Kundera described: a freedom from gravity, a release from the weight of effort, skill or limitation. For a moment, the digital world seemed almost enchanted. Who would not enjoy the idea of having a small, tireless companion capable of producing endless text, images, and analysis at the speed of thought? It was fun. It was fascinating. It was power without responsibility.

We humans have never been particularly good at resisting magic, especially the cheap kind. And AI, in those early encounters, revealed itself as the cheapest magic of all: infinite tricks for the price of a prompt.

But lightness, true, unanchored lightness, has a habit of floating away from meaning. And after the collective honeymoon with AI ended, we began to feel the pull of gravity again. Because on this new continent, the terrain was not ours. We were newcomers, explorers perhaps, but not the ones who owned the soil.

And owners, as history teaches us, always matter.

I grew up with computers long before any of this felt dangerous. Back then I used a 2400-baud modem, a relic few remember anymore. Two hundred characters per second, if the line was clean and nobody in your house picked up the phone. Slow enough that you could almost feel each letter walking its way onto the screen. But still, humans max out their fingers at fifteen characters per second, so it was impressive.

But the slowness was never a problem. Before websites existed, I played chess on BBS boards with strangers scattered across the world, to the distress of my father and his phone bill. I never knew who they were, age, background, beliefs, but that was part of the freedom. It was dangerous in theory, yet completely without judgment. No discrimination. No profiles. No targeted anything. Just two humans moving pieces across a shared digital board, connected only by curiosity and a squealing modem. The internet was open, ungoverned, and wild in every direction. Light in the best and worst sense of the word. It was a place where you could build anything, break anything, and explore everything without asking permission from anyone. There were dark corners, of course, plenty of them, but there was fairness in the chaos. No emperor, no gatekeeper, no algorithm weighing your worth.

I am often sad to see how cheaply some of that early openness was converted into raw material, packaged and sold. The ungoverned space we once roamed freely became, quietly and systematically, a commodity. Behavioural data, what we clicked, when we paused, what made us come back (and go away), turned out to be worth more than the services themselves. Harvard professor Shoshana Zuboff called this surveillance capitalism: human experience repackaged as prediction products and sold to whoever would pay.[2] And yet I am equally relieved to see that rules, when they are made by people with values, actually work.

For more than thirty years I have worked to protect people's knowledge. And I still find myself reminding people that privacy matters even when they believe they have nothing to hide. We walk around with microphones, cameras, motion sensors and location trackers in our pockets, tiny surveillance devices we have willingly bought ourselves, and pay for each month.

In effect, we pay someone to collect knowledge about us.

If knowledge creates intelligence and intelligence creates autonomy, then controlling knowledge is, in many ways, governing autonomy itself.

Because freedom without sovereignty, I have learned, is simply permission granted by someone else. And permission can always be withdrawn.

To understand sovereignty in the age of AI, I ask you to envision a simple scene. A university decides to automate a few tasks, harmless things at first. Sorting applicants. Distributing workload. Flagging

2 Shoshana Zuboff, *The Age of Surveillance Capitalism: The Fight for a Human Future at the New Frontier of Power* (New York: PublicAffairs, 2019).

students who might need support. The systems are quick, polite, and tirelessly confident.

Until one day they are not.

An applicant disappears from a shortlist. A staff member receives an impossible schedule. A student is categorised in a way that makes no sense. Excluded. When the university asks why, the answer is a polite shrug: the system cannot say. It does not reason. It only outputs. Who knows the system, if even the people who created the models behind it are clueless?

And when models disagree with themselves, flagging the same sentence as 'harmful' one day and 'harmless' the next, authority turns arbitrary. That is not a glitch; it is what happens when judgment is outsourced to systems we cannot question.

That moment, when responsibility remains human but authority has shifted somewhere else, is where sovereignty suddenly becomes more than a word. It becomes a practical necessity. A reminder that even on a new planet, you must know who owns the ground beneath your feet.

If you want to own something, you cannot stay invisible. Someone has to know who you are, or ownership dissolves into no one's problem. A little weight, identity, accountability, is what makes lightness meaningful.

And owning the ground is not just about where servers sit. A promise of 'local' means little if another country can compel access. A vendor may offer residency; jurisdiction decides who can knock on the door.

The West, the East, and Europe are playing different games on the same field. The EU's GDPR limits what can be collected; the US CLOUD Act determines who can demand it; China's data laws keep it inside borders that serve the state. Knowing whose court you are on matters, especially when the referees are the corporations that own the data and the infrastructure.

Will data centres on our own soil make data safe if we cannot get to it when it counts? A flag on the building is not enough if the keys belong to someone else.

The early years of AI were driven by those with the investments and resources to train enormous models on huge clusters of processors and oceans of data. Everyone else became users. And users, no matter how clever, do not write the rules.

It was a quiet shift of power: dependency disguised as innovation, lightness disguised as freedom. The world moves forward quickly, but not always in a direction chosen by the people living in it. Everybody needs to get on the train before it leaves, but nobody is asking where the train is going.

When an AI system creates something, an image, a melody, a sentence, it feels new. But it is new only in the way a remix is new. AI learns by absorbing our collective memory. And this raises a dangerous question: who gets to learn from culture, and who gets to profit from it?

Pattern recognition is not creativity, but combining different patterns could be. User input is needed for anything new to happen. But users combining unrelated patterns can lead to unpredictable results. Some fascinating and innovative, some atrocious and hopefully laughable.

There is a quieter misunderstanding at work here. Pattern recognition teaches us about the past; it does not tell the future. Models learn what has happened often enough to look stable. They are excellent at describing yesterday, and very confident while doing so. But the future is where patterns break. New ideas, new movements, new risks rarely announce themselves in familiar shapes. When we let systems trained on history decide what comes next, we risk mistaking repetition for foresight. Prediction becomes momentum, and momentum starts to look like inevitability. That is not intelligence; it is inertia, dressed up as insight.

We understand this intuitively about ourselves. Every time we use our brain for something new, it grows. Every time we repeat a thought, it gets stronger. Habits form. Shortcuts harden. The same logic applies to learning machines. If a model continues to learn from interaction, then usage becomes training, whether we intend it or not. And not every user is a good teacher. Repeated patterns, jokes, abuse, simplifications, or biases do not stay at the surface; they sink in. Given enough repetition, they begin to look like the truth.

Some early AI systems were taken offline not because they were technically broken, but because exposure to how people treated them warped their behaviour beyond repair. 'Tay' lasted fewer than sixteen hours online before it had to be quietly switched off. Not because it had failed, but precisely because it had succeeded. It had learned exactly what it was taught.[3] Deployment is not the end of responsibility; it is the moment it truly begins.

So far unique internationally, Norway's government has agreed to subsidize media for AI training on their data, and training has a price tag: 45 million NOK a year to let new AI models learn from all the editor-verified newspaper content older than one year, with money flowing back to the creators to justify the use. It is a negotiated license over the nation's memory: yes to archives, no to the freshest news, a deliberate fence around what can be mined. Sovereignty is not abstract, it is a contract that says culture is not just 'data', and access is earned, not assumed.[4]

Europe has already drawn lines here too: text and data mining is not a free-for-all, and training on copyrighted work is not automatically 'learning'. Music platforms argue it is fair use and inevitability; creators see their voices turned into features. If sovereignty means owning your own stories, then governing training data is part of the job. Those who had profited most from copyright were suddenly very interested in these questions, but the answers lagged far behind the concern.

Some creators were shocked to discover their life's work recognised in models they never agreed to train. And on a macro level, entire populations have seen their personal data profiled, repackaged, and used to classify them in ways they never intended. Sometimes excluded in the same profiling, which could be worse, depending on the case at hand.

The Cambridge Analytica scandal made this concrete. Up to 87 million Facebook users had their personal data harvested without consent, turned into psychological profiles, and used for political targeting, by a firm most of them had never heard of, for purposes they had never imagined.[5] They had not been hacked. They had simply been users.

---

3 Microsoft Official Blog, 'Learning from Tay's Introduction', 25 March 2016, https://blogs.microsoft.com/blog/2016/03/25/learning-tays-introduction/

4 Nasjonalbiblioteket, 'Regjeringen vil styrke norsk kunstig intelligens med 45 millioner', *Nasjonalbiblioteket*, 2 September 2025, https://www.nb.no/nyheter/regjeringen-vil-styrke-norsk-kunstig-intelligens-med-45-millioner/

5 Carole Cadwalladr and Emma Graham-Harrison, 'Revealed: 50 Million Facebook Profiles Harvested for Cambridge Analytica in Major Data Breach', *The Guardian*, 17 March 2018, https://www.theguardian.com/news/2018/mar/17/cambridge-analytica-facebook-influence-us-election

Corporations have bought and sold rights to media for decades. What will their price be for training material? Already we are seeing brokered deals in mainstream media where popular brands are outsourcing their trademarks to AI vendors.

Too often, gains are kept private while the harms are spread thin. Profit is owned; loss is socialised.

This is the quiet breaking of our limits, these moments where openness becomes extraction, where the wild frontier becomes fenced land. Others argue that learning is universal, humans learn from everything; why should not machines? But machines learn at a scale that no human ever could, with an efficiency no artist can compete with.

And who owns the machine?

This is where sovereignty stops being political and becomes cultural. A society that cannot govern the use of its own stories, risks losing control of its future voice.

Europe chose a heavier path. Not to slow innovation, but to anchor it.

Instead of allowing AI to drift into unregulated territory, or reacting with fear, Europe insisted that technology shaping people's lives must obey the values of the societies it serves.

The EU AI Act[6] puts weight where it matters: systems that influence rights must be open to challenge, emotion recognition in classrooms and workplaces is out of bounds, and synthetic content should be marked as such. Those are not compliance chores; they're design constraints. They force builders to keep humans in the loop, to prove provenance, and to accept that some uses are simply off limits. That is sovereignty with teeth.

If the regulations we need move slower than the systems we build, we are sailing on judgment and values. Without them, there is no heading at all.

People say these rules are heavy. Perhaps they are. But I have also seen the alternative: personal data misused, identities reduced to behavioural predictions, human judgment replaced by automated certainty. The weight of rules may slow us down, yes, but it also stops us from sliding into places we should never go.

I have seen the good side too: people sharing knowledge openly,

6 See https://www.europarl.europa.eu/thinktank/en/document/EPRS_BRI(2021)698792

people learning to classify and protect their information, asking themselves whether something is private, sensitive or open. Learning that encryption is not dangerous. What do you post online? Which apps do you use? What do you tell the robot? Small acts, but it is the beginning of sovereignty.

Perhaps the rules are heavy. But weight is not the opposite of freedom. Weight is what gives freedom shape. But we also need the light.

Innovation is the light we need in order to grow. It lets ideas travel fast, cross borders, and combine in ways we could not plan in advance. But light without gravity does not nourish anything; it just drifts. Regulation is the weight that pulls innovation into fertile soil, where it can take root and feed more than itself. Uninhibited growth becomes a cancer, consuming the systems it depends on. Rules that cannot be challenged by change, on the other hand, harden into something else entirely. They stop protecting and start controlling. The balance between light and weight cannot be fixed once and for all; it has to remain dynamic. If we want progress without stagnation, innovation without harm, we must be willing to continuously revisit and revise the rulebook that holds it in place.

This is responsibility.

Kundera writes about kitsch, beauty without truth. Emotion without complexity. Comfort without thought, a sentimental imitation of beauty that strips away complexity. On Planet Internet, kitsch has found its home.

AI can create beautiful illusions: speeches that feel wise, faces that feel familiar, memories that feel real. But beauty without burden is hollow. A deepfake smile travels farther than a genuine one. A neatly summarised lie outruns a messy truth. A synthetic history, repeated often enough, becomes cultural memory.

Without provenance and governance, that memory hardens into someone else's narrative. Weight here is marking what is synthetic, challenging what is flat, and refusing to let repetition stand in for truth.

My grandmother never trusted calculators. She was working in a convenience store using pencil and paper for writing receipts. The machines came, and she, reluctantly, was forced to use them. She would always put in the numbers, then look up, and say 'mm', as if she was sceptical, but approving. Every answer was double-checked in her head. She trusted her own mind more than any machine. A lesson I did not appreciate back then, but one I think about often now.

We should challenge our perception, and look under the hood.

Transparency is not there to ruin the magic. It is there to preserve meaning.

Without weight, everything becomes decoration, and decoration cannot guide a society.

A Norwegian developer noticed the same pattern in our own history: when the Bronze Age reached Norway, power belonged to the few who controlled trade in imported metals.[7] Everyone else depended on them.

The parallel to AI is exact. If the Bronze Age concentrated power, the Iron Age distributed it. Not because iron was simpler, but because knowledge spread.

Call the last decade our Digital Bronze Age: advanced AI was the domain of a global elite with massive data centres and armies of specialists. Like bronze that had to be imported and controlled by a few families, this AI was closed, expensive, and shaped elsewhere. The emerging Digital Iron Age looks different. Iron was the 'democratic metal' because people learned to pull it from local bog ore; power shifted when the knowledge spread. Open models that we can run on our own hardware are that shift. They make AI knowledge common property, *allemannseie*. In Norway, the right to roam nature freely is defined by law: the Outdoor Recreation Act of 1957 holds that land belongs to no one and everyone at once. The right to roam knowledge should be no different.

Today you can run surprisingly large models on a laptop. Sovereignty is technically within reach, but is it accessible? The digital divide is priced in currency. Who can afford the hardware, the power, the bandwidth.

But running is not the same as training. Fine-tuning a model on your own data, the step that turns a general tool into a sovereign one, still demands expertise and compute that few institutions command. The Iron Age metaphor holds, but only if we invest in spreading the craft, not just distributing the ore.

A digital Iron Age means open infrastructure, public computing capacity, transparent systems when possible, and collaboration across

7 'Slik bygger vi en fremtid der kunstig intelligens blir en ressurs for fellesskapet'. See Tore André Rosander, 'Advarer mot AI-gigantene: – Vi mister kontroll, bremser verdiskaping', *kode24*, 15 September 2025, https://www.kode24.no/artikkel/advarer-mot-ai-gigantene-vi-mister-kontroll-bremser-verdiskaping/245309

disciplines and borders, not just engineers, but ethicists, artists, educators, public servants.

It means nations and institutions have choices. It means society can steer. It means we stop outsourcing our values to distant systems.

Kundera asked whether we should choose lightness or weight. AI makes the answer clear: we need both. Lightness for imagination and possibility. Weight for responsibility and truth.

Planet Internet is still young. Its borders are fluid, its powers unfinished, its values not yet fully declared. And the bandwidth that fuels it is almost comic when compared to our own human pace. A 1-Gbps connection can send 125 million characters per second, entire libraries in moments, while we sit here typing letters one by one with clumsy fingers on screens that autocorrect half our thoughts.

The imbalance between machine speed and human intention is astonishing, but not hopeless. Corporations rarely change their internal laws unless it threatens their bottom line. Every continent is a market. Every law is a boundary to work through. That is the reality of power. But power is not destiny. We still have the chance to shape this digital planet before it hardens.

The future will be built by those who are light enough to explore... and heavy enough to steer.

Kasparov lost to Deep Blue in 1997. Lee Sedol lost to AlphaGo in 2016. Both walked away knowing the rules had changed. What neither match settled was who gets to write the next ones.

The Iron Age did not arrive because someone powerful decided to share. It arrived because ordinary people learned to find iron in their own bogs, on their own terms. That knowledge could not be taxed or embargoed. It simply spread.

We are at the same threshold. The models exist. The knowledge is spreading. The question is not whether we can build a Digital Iron Age. It is whether we will choose to. Whether nations, institutions, and individuals will pick up the tools available to them, or wait for permission from those who would rather we remained users.

Sovereignty is not isolation. It is the ability to stand upright and say yes, or no, on your own terms.

And the only unbearable thing would be pretending we have no choice.

AI DISCLAIMER: In the writing of this chapters, the author has used AI tools for organization of information and research, and for analysis of text and feedback. The written text is his own and not AI-generated.

References

Cadwalladr, Carole, and Emma Graham-Harrison, 'Revealed: 50 Million Facebook Profiles Harvested for Cambridge Analytica in Major Data Breach', *The Guardian*, 17 March 2018, https://www.theguardian.com/news/2018/mar/17/cambridge-analytica-facebook-influence-us-election

Kundera, Milan, *The Book of Laughter and Forgetting*, trans. by Michael Henry Heim (New York: Alfred A. Knopf, 1980).

Microsoft Official Blog, 'Learning from Tay's Introduction', 25 March 2016, https://blogs.microsoft.com/blog/2016/03/25/learning-tays-introduction/

Nasjonalbiblioteket, *'Regjeringen vil styrke norsk kunstig intelligens med 45 millioner'*, *Nasjonalbiblioteket*, 2 September 2025, https://www.nb.no/nyheter/regjeringen-vil-styrke-norsk-kunstig-intelligens-med-45-millioner/

Rosander, Tore André, 'Advarer mot AI-gigantene: – Vi mister kontroll, bremser verdiskaping', *kode24*, 15 September 2025, https://www.kode24.no/artikkel/advarer-mot-ai-gigantene-vi-mister-kontroll-bremser-verdiskaping/245309

Zuboff, Shoshana, *The Age of Surveillance Capitalism: The Fight for a Human Future at the New Frontier of Power* (New York: PublicAffairs, 2019).

2. Sustainable AI

Laura Maria Ferri and Cal Innes

Part 1. Sustainability Concerns Surrounding AI

The Price of Progress

Artificial intelligence is rapidly transforming our world. But it is becoming increasingly clear that this transformation comes with a tangible impact on our environment; one that merits our immediate attention. When, for example, we ask a chatbot like ChatGPT or Claude a question, the interaction may feel deceptively simple; instantaneous text appearing on a screen as if by magic. Yet, like all magic tricks, its impressiveness is reliant on something the audience cannot see. In this case, what we cannot see is a vast infrastructure of servers, cooling systems, and global supply chains; each consuming resources at a scale and pace that we cannot, or rather should not ignore.

Understanding and addressing these impacts is not about rejecting AI, but about approaching the issue with clarity around the facts, and a sense of moral responsibility regarding the outcomes of our digital actions. If we are to integrate this technology responsibly into our institutions and wider societies, it is essential that we are honest and upfront about its true environmental costs and benefits. Only then can we truly appreciate the magic without being blinded by it.

Energy and Carbon

When we talk about the energy footprint of artificial intelligence, it helps to look closely at where that energy actually goes. Broadly speaking,

 https://doi.org/10.11647/OBP.0530.02

this can be broken down into two phases. The first is training, which is the process of building a large language model. This is an energy-intensive task, but it usually only happens once, or perhaps a few times during occasional updates. The second phase is inference, which occurs every time a system responds to a query, produces a recommendation, or generates an output. Although each inference requires much less energy, it happens far more frequently. As artificial intelligence becomes more deeply woven into the services we rely on, the energy consumed by inference in many cases outweighs the energy required for training.[1]

This matters because artificial intelligence now operates across an enormous range of applications; from the growing number of chatbots and image generators that have captured public attention to the less obvious models running in the background of everyday life, filtering social media content, guiding delivery vehicles, and running security checks on our bank transactions.

To put this into perspective, the 2025 Stanford AI Index Report offers some useful comparisons. Generating a single image using an AI model consumes roughly the same amount of energy as fully charging a smartphone.

A text-based query to a large language model uses around ten times more energy than a standard web search. These may sound modest in isolation, but when multiplied across billions of daily interactions worldwide, the cumulative demand becomes significant. According to the same report, the computational power used to train frontier AI models is now doubling approximately every five months, far outpacing improvements in hardware efficiency.[2]

And this is only the beginning. These systems are increasing in size and complexity. Artificial intelligence is appearing in more digital tools, such as search engines, email services, navigation apps and streaming platforms. As capabilities improve, usage rises to meet them. The question is no longer whether energy demand will increase due to the

---

1 International Energy Agency, *Electricity 2024: Analysis and Forecast to 2026* (Paris: IEA, 2024, https://www.iea.org/reports/electricity-2024; see also MIT Technology Review, 'Power Hungry: AI and Our Energy Future', 2025, https://www.technologyreview.com/supertopic/ai-energy-package/

2 N. Maslej, L. Fattorini, R. Perrault et al., *Artificial Intelligence Index Report 2025* (Stanford, CA: Stanford Institute for Human-Centered AI, 2025), https://hai.stanford.edu/ai-index/2025-ai-index-report

proliferation of AI, but how sharply it will rise in the years ahead.

There are numerous factors that contribute to the amount of energy required to run these systems, such as model size, the complexity of the task, and hardware efficiency. But one of the most significant is geography. The carbon impact linked to this growth varies enormously depending on where the computation takes place. A data centre powered by renewable energy in Norway, for example, leaves a very different mark on the atmosphere than one connected to a more fossil fuel-dependent grid in countries like China, India or the United States. Yet in practice, the placement of data centres is often driven by land prices, tax rules and proximity to users rather than environmental considerations like the carbon intensity of local power supplies. This creates an unsettling mismatch. The environmental footprint of artificial intelligence is shaped not only by how much energy it uses, but by the choices behind where that energy comes from.

Water

While energy tends to dominate the conversation about AI's environmental footprint, the technology's growing demand for water deserves equal attention. Data centres, because of the intense electrical load required to run modern servers, produce a large amount of heat, and many rely on evaporative cooling systems to keep servers stable. This method uses significant volumes of fresh water, often drawn from the same finite supplies that nearby communities depend on.

The exact amount of water varies considerably by climate, data centre design, and task. But overall the pattern is clear. As artificial intelligence workloads grow, water consumption grows with them. Some of the larger facilities now use enough water every day to meet the needs of thousands of households.[3]

Here too, geography plays a decisive role. Many data centres are located in areas already facing concerning levels of water scarcity,

3 Wesley Spindler, Luna Atamian Hahn-Petersen and Sadaf Hosseini, 'Circular Water Solutions Key to Sustainable Data Centres', *World Economic Forum*, 7 November 2024, https://www.weforum.org/stories/2024/11/circular-water-solutions-sustainable-data-centres/; see also Ren Shaolei, and Amy Luers, 'The Real Story on AI Water Usage at Data Centers', *IEEE Spectrum*, 10 September 2025, https://spectrum.ieee.org/ai-water-usage

which places added pressure on communities that are often least able to cope with it. In some regions, proposals for new facilities have, understandably, sparked strong local resistance, largely because the projected water use would stretch supplies that residents rely on.

This is not a distant or hypothetical risk. Artificial intelligence contributes to rising energy demand, which contributes to the emissions that drive climate change, which in turn intensifies droughts and disrupts water systems. In other words, the infrastructure built to support artificial intelligence can worsen the very pressures that make water harder to secure, creating a very dangerous and very real environmental feedback loop.

Materials and Waste

The environmental impact of artificial intelligence begins long before a model is trained or a query is answered. The servers, processors and networking systems that support these technologies depend on global supply chains that draw on rare earth elements and other critical minerals. Mining these materials often damages ecosystems, pollutes waterways and generates significant greenhouse gas emissions. There is also a human cost. The communities that bear the environmental and health consequences of extraction are seldom, if ever, the ones who benefit most from the technologies they enable. Reports of unsafe working conditions, child labour and exploitative practices make it clear that questions around the sustainability of AI are a social concern as much as an environmental one.

But it is not just the ways in which these systems are created which is cause for concern. At the other end of the lifecycle lies the growing challenge of electronic waste. Artificial intelligence systems evolve quickly, and the hardware that powers them usually becomes outdated significantly faster than traditional computing equipment.[4] The constant need for greater speed and efficiency drives rapid replacement cycles, and a significant portion of the discarded hardware becomes waste.

4 Peng Wang, Ling-Yu Zhang, Asaf Tzachor and Wei-Qiang Chen, 'E-waste Challenges of Generative Artificial Intelligence', *Nat Comput Sci*, 4 (2024), 818–823, https://doi.org/10.1038/s43588-024-00712-6

Globally, only a small share of this waste is recycled through formal, safe channels. According to the UN e-waste monitor, more than three quarters of electronic waste ends up in landfills, incinerators or informal processing sites where workers are exposed to hazardous materials without adequate protection.[5] As adoption expands, the volume of specialised hardware requiring disposal will inevitably grow. Without substantial advances in recycling infrastructure and long-term product design, this problem will sadly continue to intensify.

Labour and Livelihoods

The environmental costs of artificial intelligence are not the only cause for concern. There is also a growing conversation about the technology's impact on employment and livelihoods. As AI systems become more capable, they are increasingly being deployed to perform tasks previously carried out by people, from customer service and content moderation to legal research and software development. While some argue this will free workers for more creative or strategic roles, others point to a more uncertain reality: displacement without clear pathways to alternative employment.

This is not a distant prospect. Major technology companies have already cited AI capabilities as a factor in workforce reductions, and recent analysis suggests that roles involving routine cognitive tasks are particularly exposed.[6] The benefits of AI-driven productivity gains, meanwhile, tend to accrue unevenly, often favouring those who own or control the systems rather than those whose labour they replace.

If artificial intelligence is to be considered truly sustainable, we must account not only for its environmental footprint but also for its effects on the people and communities whose working lives it reshapes.

---

5 United Nations, *Global E-Waste Monitor 2024*, https://ewastemonitor.info/

6 Maslej, Fattorini, Perrault et al., *Artificial Intelligence Index Report 2025*; see also Mauro Cazzaniga, Florence Jaumotte, Longji Li, Giovanni Melina et al., 'Gen-AI: Artificial Intelligence and the Future of Work', *International Monetary Fund* (2024), https://www.imf.org/en/Publications/Staff-Discussion-Notes/Issues/2024/01/14/Gen-AI-Artificial-Intelligence-and-the-Future-of-Work-542379

Signs of Progress?

The picture we have painted so far is undeniably bleak, yet it is not without the possibility of meaningful change. There are real reasons to believe that the environmental footprint of artificial intelligence can be reduced, even as adoption grows and its environmental effects become clearer.

Hardware is improving at a steady pace. Each new generation of processors delivers more computing power for the same amount of, and in some cases less, energy. This is the result of deliberate engineering progress and strong competitive pressure. At the same time, researchers are developing smaller and more efficient models that challenge the idea that bigger is always better. Techniques such as model compression and more selective training are reducing energy demands without sacrificing performance.

There are also signs of progress within the infrastructure itself. Some data centre operators are adopting closed-loop cooling systems that greatly reduce water use. Others are making efforts to source more of their electricity from renewable energy, although progress remains uneven and sometimes overstated. New regulatory requirements are beginning to emerge as well. In the European Union, for example, operators are now required to report their energy and water use, which introduces a level of transparency that may encourage better practice across the industry.[7]

Even with these developments, we should be cautious not to celebrate our achievements too soon. Efficiency gains can be overtaken by rising demand, a pattern seen time and time again in other sectors in recent history. Yet the future is not predetermined. The choices made now by developers, operators, institutions and regulators will shape whether the environmental impact of artificial intelligence is managed responsibly or allowed to grow beyond our ability to respond in time.

Every institution and individual who develops, deploys or even simply uses AI-powered tools and systems has both an opportunity and a moral obligation to consider, and hopefully address, these impacts.

7 European Union, *Energy Efficiency Directive (EED) 2024*, https://energy.ec.europa.eu/topics/energy-efficiency/energy-efficiency-targets-directive-and-rules/energy-efficiency-directive_en

The goal is not to slow progress, but to approach it with care and deliberation. This means measuring what we use, disclosing what we find and acting on what we learn. Only then can we enjoy the magic of AI without leaving future generations to deal with the environmental cost that lies hidden behind the curtain.

Part 2. AI-empowered Sustainability

After discussing the 'dark side' of AI and the environmental and social costs embedded in its lifecycle, this chapter turns into its 'bright side', highlighting how it can support the achievement of sustainability-related goals.

While AI has enormous downsides, it also has the potential to become a powerful agent for positive change and serve the aim of boosting our ability to tackle some of the most relevant societal challenges. Whereas the use of AI requires large amounts of natural resources, its integration into production systems could, on the other side, elevate the operations planning capabilities, minimise errors, improve predictions or lighten the workload through better distribution of tasks. On the social side, well-trained AI-powered systems could facilitate the overcoming of barriers to service access, increase the understanding of underlying dynamics of a social problem, and support more inclusive and effective policy making. However, it is important to keep in mind that the two sides are strictly interdependent: an AI tool which aims at creating, for instance, positive social impact but is highly polluting will not reach its full potential as it will simultaneously create and destroy value on the two different dimensions.

Undoubtedly, the problem today is not whether AI and sustainable and responsible development are intertwined—that is abundantly evident—but how we should govern and manage them so that they can generate reciprocal improvements. And although it seems obvious, we do not have answers yet and no consensus exist on how AI could advance sustainability in an equitable and effective way. The question is complex, as it involves organisational arrangements, institutional commitments, political choices and cultural values.

Most of the studies and discussions have so far focused on investigating the 'dark side', exploring the many negative impacts of its lifecycle and related costs, but much less evidence exists on how it is contributing to reach better solutions to societal problems. AI technologies and devices are already transforming the society at macro (social system), meso (organisational level) and micro (individual) level, but how they are harnessed to form and support societal transformation and contribute to the cause of sustainable development is still overlooked. The good news is that exemplars are emerging that blaze a trail: just to cite a few, AI technologies are supporting the innovation of healthcare processes improving the diagnostic capacity (see Chapter 5 in this volume); as well, AI tools are being integrated with educational services, thus enhancing accessibility (see Chapter 9 in this volume) and performance; and they are also being adopted in manufacturing processes to allow better resource allocation and planning.[8]

It is almost impossible to summarise and discuss each and every AI application here, but the following discussion will try and give an overview of the different areas and many opportunities that can arise from a conscious management of AI and sustainability integration. It is an intricate journey because AI and sustainability concepts and practices are in constant transformation and their integration is rooted in ever faster innovation capacity.[9] Accordingly, it requires more than just the successful application of AI tools to the management of social or environmental processes; it may require the ability and willingness to change and revise how AI tools are trained and developed, how social and environmental goals are defined and, to some extent, it may also lead to limits and constraints to AI development, on the basis of ethical considerations.

AI as a Tool vs AI as an Agent for Sustainability

It is well known that we can give AI different roles, spanning from a 'simple' tool for operational support, to an assistant that performs

8 Rakibul Hasan Chowdhury, 'AI-driven Business Analytics for Operational Efficiency', *World Journal of Advanced Engineering Technology and Sciences*, 12.2 (2024), 535–543. See also https://www.ibm.com/think/topics/ai-in-operations-management

9 Stefano Belletti, *Verde & Digitale. In viaggio tra sostenibilità, innovazione e competitività* (Milan: Edizioni Ambiente, 2022).

specific tasks without our direct supervision, to an agent which is able to (pro)actively act as partner in problem solving and decision-making.[10] Moving away from the discussion about how we should frame human–AI interaction, which is a very interesting debate but outside the scope of the present contribution, the difference lies in the trade-off between human control and AI effectiveness and rapidity. It implies an accurate evaluation of the social and environmental challenges we are considering and the impact that we aim to generate, together with the potential challenges our stakeholders may have to face: AI as a tool can support our decisions and actions through advanced data analytics, predictive insights and improved productivity; AI as an agent engages in more autonomous collaboration such as self-directed problem-solving, which opens a broader set of opportunities, but increases the risks of biases, lack of supervision and transparency. The choice is in our hands and we have no one-size-fits-all solutions. The relevant use of AI depends on the specific nature of the social and environmental challenge we are tackling, how this challenge relates to the life and conditions of the targeted stakeholders and how strategic it is to support the sustainable development of the population, how able we are to address all key dimensions, the breadth and depth of the problems, etc. Our point here is that social and environmental issues require more than technical and quantitative approaches; they need qualitative evaluation and critical thinking as they generate direct and indirect effects on societal and individual conditions, they have ethical implications and they affect future development. Hence, keeping humans in the loop to guarantee supervision and expertise, without leaving the decision and implementation of solutions to AI agent autonomy is of paramount importance to identify the best direction to follow towards the sustainable development and is strategic to guarantee that AI-empowered sustainability is genuinely oriented to social good[11] and human centricity.

---

10 Emanuele Farri and Gianluca Rosani, *HBR Guide to Generative AI for Managers* (Cornwall: Harvard Business School Publishing Corporation, 2025).

11 Luciano Floridi, *The Ethics of Artificial Intelligence: Principles, Challenges, and Opportunities* (Oxford: Oxford University Press, 2023).

AI and Sustainable Development Goals (SDGs)

The lens that we will use to provide insights on AI-empowered sustainability opportunities is derived from the UN Sustainable Development Goals (SDGs), a set of seventeen goals and 169 targets set by the UN back in 2015 and representing 'a universal call to action to end poverty, protect the planet, and ensure that by 2030 all people enjoy peace and prosperity'.[12] Acknowledging the crucial role of digital technologies, the United Nations Development Programme (UNDP) has recently published the *SDG Digital Acceleration Agenda* to explore how they are already being used and can be scaled further in order to offer a positive contribution towards achieving the SDGs.[13] Showcasing thirty-four digital solutions, the document is a useful guide on how to apply digital technologies—AI among them—as enablers of sustainability commitments. Looking at AI, the study underlines how it has the potential to create paradigm shifts in the trajectory of sustainable development, especially in low- and middle-income societies.

Extant literature has explored the application of AI in achieving SDGs and results are mixed and inconsistent. From a general perspective, studies reveal that progress has been made, but it is overestimated.[14] Of course, advancements in machine learning, data analytics and automation increased the 'potential of AI to address challenges such as climate change, poverty, and healthcare', however we are today still far from having ecosystems and models really able to lead an AI-empowered sustainable future.[15]

Delving into the possible AI applications to SDGs, the following discussion is organised in three parts according to the three main pillars of sustainability, namely environmental, social and economic. Accordingly, though SDGs are not classified using these three dimensions, we will

---

12 United Nations Development Programme, *Sustainable Development Goals*, https://www.undp.org/united-states/sustainable-development-goals

13 See https://www.sdg-digital.org/

14 Amarjit J. Meitei, Pradeep Rai and S. S. Rajkishan, 'Application of AI/ML Techniques in Achieving SDGs: A Bibliometric Study', *Environment, Development and Sustainability*, 27 (2023), 281–317, https://doi.org/10.1007/s10668-023-03935-1

15 Lucas Greif, Fabian Röckel, Andreas Kimmig and Jivka Ovtcharova, 'A Systematic Review of Current AI Techniques Used in the Context of the SDGs', *International Journal of Environmental Research*, 19 (2025), Article 1, https://doi.org/10.1007/s41742-024-00668-5, p. 20

consider the dimension that is more closely related and prevalent. The topic is extremely fascinating but equally extensive and complex, hence the following paragraphs aim at outlining a synthetic analysis to provide a useful reference for further advancements.

AI Applications to Environmental SDGs

Environmental impact remains the most established and mature area of application for AI within the broader sustainability agenda. Broadening the perspective for a moment, a study conducted by market research company Ipsos and the European Commission on the contribution of Information and Communications Technology to the environmental sustainability efforts of EU enterprises reports that '60% of those using collaborative [platforms] stated [...] environmental sustainability as a motivation for their choice. Similarly, 55% of those using AI, and 58% of those using cloud computing cited environmental reasons'.[16] This suggests that digital technologies and AI are widely regarded as essential enablers of corporate environmental commitments, helping set the pace for sustainability-oriented innovation.

A growing body of research has examined how major corporations deploy AI to achieve energy savings, enhance eco-efficiency, or support humanitarian initiatives such as disaster relief.[17] Existing evidence primarily highlights uses related to resource minimisation, energy and water conservation, environmental monitoring and risk prediction, and the simulation of ecological conditions. More advanced approaches are emerging as well, including autonomous systems capable of planning and executing interventions such as optimised resource allocation or real-time modelling for disaster anticipation and response.

The following table outlines illustrative examples of AI-enabled applications aligned with each of the Sustainable Development Goals (SDGs).

---

16 European Commission, *Survey on the Contribution of ICT to the Environmental Sustainability of Actions of EU Enterprises* (Luxembourg: Publications Office of the European Union, 2021), https://digital-strategy.ec.europa.eu/en/library/survey-contribution-ict-environmental-sustainability-actions-eu-enterprises

17 José M. Ferres, William B. Week and Bradley Smith, *AI for Good: Applications in Sustainability, Humanitarian Action, and Health* (Hoboken, NJ: John Wiley & Sons, 2024).

Table 2.1 Examples of AI-enabled applications aligned with each SDG.

SDG	Goal	AI as tool	AI as agent
6	Clean Water and Sanitation	Water quality monitoring with smart sensors.	Robots that inspect pipes, sewers, and water facilities, flagging anomalies.
7	Affordable and Clean Energy	Energy consumption optimisation and predictive maintenance.	Distributed agents in grid components that negotiate load, storage, and pricing.
12	Responsible Consumption and Production	Predictive models on waste generation and minimisation solutions.	Autonomous just-in-time reordering; agents learning user habits and optimising without manual input.
13	Climate Action	Nowcasting and scenario analysis. Drones monitoring and mapping biodiversity changes in climate-vulnerable areas.	Autonomous emergency response through robots and sensors for real-time risk mitigation or interventions.
14	Life Below Water	Sensors and data analytics to constantly monitor marine species and sea acidification levels.	Autonomous ROV/AUV for monitoring and clean-up of underwater landscape.
15	Life on Land	AI-powered digital twins for realistic and interactive 3D models to integrate ecosystem and biodiversity values into national and local planning.	Multi-agent systems for wildfire management and mitigation interventions planning.

AI Applications to Social SDGs

Growing efforts to develop AI applications for environmental sustainability are well established, but recent years have also seen a marked rise in attention toward AI for social good.[18] A study by McKinsey indicates that institutions, businesses and non-profit organisations increasingly adopt AI tools as enablers of social-impact initiatives across the full spectrum of the Sustainable Development Goals (SDGs).[19] Their findings suggest that AI solutions are perceived as particularly impactful in advancing Good Health and Well-Being (SDG 3) and Quality Education (SDG 4). This trend is echoed by the World Economic Forum, which identifies healthcare and education among the top social-impact domains for AI applications.[20] AI is also emerging as a catalyst for social innovation, enhancing the accessibility and inclusivity of products and services. Its perceived transformative potential lies in the ability to address complex societal challenges that have proven resistant to previous technological approaches.

However, compared with the environmental dimension, the social dimension of sustainability is especially sensitive to persistent limitations in AI development and deployment, most notably issues of bias, ethics and contextual applicability. Many socially oriented goals are hindered by unequal representation of demographic groups in training datasets (e.g., gender or racial biases in healthcare), with disparities varying significantly across countries. These gaps undermine the reliability, fairness, and scalability of AI systems. Ethical concerns are also intensifying as AI becomes more generative and autonomous, underscoring the need for robust ethical design and governance frameworks. Finally, while environmental challenges can often be addressed through technical optimisation, social challenges inherently require human interaction, empathy, and contextual understanding. This makes it more difficult for AI systems to fully capture

---

18 Nenad Tomašev et al., 'AI for Social Good: Unlocking the Opportunity for Positive Impact', *Nature Communications*, 11 (2020), 2468, https://doi.org/10.1038/s41467-020-15871-z

19 McKinsey and Company, 'AI for Social Good: Improving Lives and Protecting the Planet', *McKinsey*, 10 May 2024, https://www.mckinsey.com/capabilities/quantumblack/our-insights/ai-for-social-good

20 World Economic Forum, *AI for Impact: The PRISM Framework for Responsible AI in Social Innovation* (Geneva: WEF, 2024), https://www.weforum.org/publications/ai-for-impact-the-prism-framework-for-responsible-ai-in-social-innovation/

the nuances of people's lived experiences and community dynamics, limiting their effectiveness and increasing implementation costs.

As per the environmental dimension, below I showcase a table with examples of possible AI tools and applications which can contribute to social SDGs.

Table 2.2 Examples of AI tools and applications contributing to social SDGs.

SDG	Goal	AI as tool	AI as agent
1	No Poverty	Predictive analytics on the evolution of social conditions and needs in poorest regions.	Semi-autonomous selection of beneficiaries and credit allocation.
2	Zero Hunger	Optimisation of agri-food supplies distribution.	Autonomous robots and agents to monitor and enhance soil conditions and agri-food productivity capacity.
3	Good Health and Well-being	AI-assisted diagnostics to improve medical image interpretations for anticipated illness detection.	Assistive AI-powered robots for remote healthcare.
4	Quality Education	Customised learning paths. Detection of patterns of risks to learning paths.	Autonomous models or tutors to enable students' progress.
5	Gender Equality	Data analysis to identify hidden or unknown patterns of violent behaviours.	Conversational agents that detect potential gender-based harassment and offer supporting solutions.
16	Peace, Justice and Strong Institutions	Real-time detection of suspicious activities or illicit financial flows.	Agents that route cases to appropriate judiciary and prosecution bodies.

AI Applications to Economic/Institutional SDGs

As AI becomes increasingly embedded in strategies, processes and models for sustainable development, its relevance in supporting the economic and institutional dimensions of SDGs is also gaining prominence. AI applications are changing how value is delivered to society and how governance mechanisms are designed, with significant impacts on societal and economic dynamics. Reports from international bodies highlight that AI has already contributed to generate progress also on SDGs mainly focused on economic and institutional topics. A major concern derives from disparities across countries, especially if we compare high-to-medium income and low-income ones, due to institutional fragility, access to infrastructure and technological literacy.[21] Coupled with AI limitations and risks, the technology's transformative potential may deepen divides rather than accelerate sustainable development, especially towards economic/institutional SDGs targets.

Table 2.3 Examples of AI applications contributing to economic/institutional SDGs.

SDG	Goal	AI as tool	AI as agent
8	Decent Work and Economic Growth	Predictive models on patterns in upskilling and reskilling priorities. Predictive analytics on accidents based on sensors.	Autonomous co-bots in production lines to substitute humans in highly risky tasks.
9	Industry, Innovation and Infrastructure	AI for R&D acceleration on materials discovery, design optimisation, and simulation.	Supervised autonomous allocation of resources to small-case enterprises in developing countries to integrate in value chains.

21 Muhammad Salar Khan, Hamza Umer and Farhana Faruqe, 'Artificial Intelligence for Low Income Countries', *Humanities and Social Sciences Communications*, 11 (2024), 1422, https://doi.org/10.1057/s41599-024-03947-w

SDG	Goal	AI as tool	AI as agent
10	Reduced Inequalities	Data analysis and modelling to simulate the impact of policies on different contexts/ different groups.	Semi-autonomous agents that proactively redirect investments where the need is greatest, in accordance to national plans and programmes.
11	Sustainable Cities and Communities	Analysis of data on transport systems to improve road safety, affordability, accessibility and sustainability.	Smart technologies that autonomously adapt spaces, lights, noise to make areas more accessible and inclusive.
17	Partnerships for the Goals	Platforms based on NLP systems to increase the accessibility of data and information from different stakeholders.	Autonomous agents that match organisations, funders, and projects based on goals and capabilities.

Concluding Remarks

The discussion above has outlined the opportunities lying behind the good government of AI to generate meaningful and equitable contributions to sustainable development. By examining key considerations and possible applications, we aimed at highlighting the systemic nature and transformative capacity of the phenomenon. On the former, the discussion underlined that AI is embedded with and interacts with a wide constellation of social, environmental, economic and institutional systems. For instance, an extensive use of AI will increase the need for energy infrastructure, which in turn will impact energy costs, land use and accessibility. In this sense, AI is not only a technological challenge, but it requires broader commitment of diverse stakeholders and multidisciplinary approaches. An AI system that delivers environmental or social benefit while generating significant emissions, consuming scarce water or displacing workers in vulnerable communities is not a clean win. Sustainable development means accounting for the full ledger, not just the outcomes we set out to achieve.

None of this is a reason for inaction. It is a reason for rigour in how we evaluate claims, design systems and decide where AI's involvement genuinely helps and where it adds complexity without adding value. The technology will continue to develop regardless. What remains in our hands is the standard we hold it to.

As for the transformative capacity of AI, previous paragraphs have discussed the potential it has to reshape processes, institutions and development trajectories in ways that advance sustainability, inclusion and equity. Concrete examples in this chapter point to real possibilities. AI is already being applied to problems that matter, from monitoring water quality to improving diagnostic accuracy to anticipating climate-related risk. The potential is genuine, and in some cases already being realised. However, potential is not the same as progress. Most of the applications described here remain in early or experimental stages, and the evidence base for AI's contribution to sustainable development is thinner than the enthusiasm surrounding it often implies. Scaling these tools equitably across different income levels, institutional capacities, and infrastructure contexts remains an unsolved problem.

Accordingly, the real possibility of AI to contribute to sustainable development and societal advancement will depend on our ability to navigate the abovementioned complexities that characterise its deployment. Hence, the future implications of AI are in our hands, and will depend on how we will shape our choices and strategies to embrace sustainable, inclusive and adaptive patterns of development, able to ensure that AI will act as catalyst of social and environmental innovations rather than an amplifier of persistent inequalities and vulnerabilities in both people and planet.

AI DISCLAIMER: C. Innes used AI as an accessibility tool to proof-read his work. Laura Maria Ferri used a conversational AI-powered assistant to support the final polishing of the manuscript. In particular, it was used to improve the English language and writing style. After using the tool, the author reviewed and edited the text and takes full responsibility for the final content.

References

Belletti, Stefano, *Verde & Digitale. In viaggio tra sostenibilità, innovazione e competitività* (Milan: Edizioni Ambiente, 2022).

Cazzaniga, Mauro, Florence Jaumotte, Longji Li, Giovanni Melina et al., 'Gen-AI: Artificial Intelligence and the Future of Work', *International Monetary Fund* (2024), https://www.imf.org/en/publications/staff-discussion-notes/issues/2024/01/14/gen-ai-artificial-intelligence-and-the-future-of-work-542379

Chowdhury, Rakibul Hasan, 'AI-driven Business Analytics for Operational Efficiency', *World Journal of Advanced Engineering Technology and Sciences*, 12.2 (2024), 535–543.

Dauvergne, Peter, *AI into the Wild. Sustainability in the Age of Artificial Intelligence* (Cambridge, MA: The MIT Press, 2020).

Dodhia, Rahul, *AI for Social Good: Using Artificial Intelligence to Save the World* (Hoboken, NJ: Wiley, 2024).

European Commission, *Survey on the Contribution of ICT to the Environmental Sustainability of Actions of EU Enterprises* (Luxembourg: Publications Office of the European Union, 2021), https://digital-strategy.ec.europa.eu/en/library/survey-contribution-ict-environmental-sustainability-actions-eu-enterprises

European Union, *Energy Efficiency Directive (EED) 2024*, https://energy.ec.europa.eu/topics/energy-efficiency/energy-efficiency-targets-directive-and-rules/energy-efficiency-directive_en

Farri, Emanuele, and Rosani, Gianluca, *HBR Guide to Generative AI for Managers* (Cornwall: Harvard Business School Publishing Corporation, 2025).

Ferres, José M., Week, William B., and Smith, Bradley, *AI for Good: Applications in Sustainability, Humanitarian Action, and Health* (Hoboken, NJ: John Wiley & Sons, 2024).

Floridi, Luciano, *The Ethics of Artificial Intelligence: Principles, Challenges, and Opportunities* (Oxford: OUP Oxford, 2023).

Greif, Lucas, Fabian Röckel, Andreas Kimmig and Jivka Ovtcharova, 'A Systematic Review of Current AI Techniques Used in the Context of the SDGs', *International Journal of Environmental Research*, 19 (2025), Article 1, https://doi.org/10.1007/s41742-024-00668-5

International Energy Agency, *Electricity 2024: Analysis and Forecast to 2026* (Paris: IEA, 2024), https://www.iea.org/reports/electricity-2024 Khan, Muhammad Salar, Hamza Umer and Farhana Faruqe, 'Artificial Intelligence for Low Income Countries', *Humanities and Social Sciences Communications*, 11 (2024), 1422, https://doi.org/10.1057/s41599-024-03947-w

McKinsey and Company, 'AI for Social Good: Improving Lives and Protecting the Planet', *McKinsey*, 10 May 2024, https://www.mckinsey.com/capabilities/quantumblack/our-insights/ai-for-social-good

Meitei, Amarjit J., Pradeep Rai, and S. S. Rajkishan, 'Application of AI/ML Techniques in Achieving SDGs: A Bibliometric Study', *Environment, Development and Sustainability*, 27 (2023), 281–317, https://doi.org/10.1007/s10668-023-03935-1

MIT Technology Review, 'Power Hungry: AI and Our Energy Future', 2025, https://www.technologyreview.com/supertopic/ai-energy-package/

Maslej, N., L. Fattorini, R. Perrault et al., *Artificial Intelligence Index Report 2025* (Stanford, CA: Stanford Institute for Human-Centered AI, 2025), https://hai.stanford.edu/ai-index/2025-ai-index-report

Ren, Shaolei, and Amy Luers, 'The Real Story on AI Water Usage at Data Centers', *IEEE Spectrum*, 10 September 2025, https://spectrum.ieee.org/ai-water-usage

Spindler, Wesley, Luna Atamian Hahn-Petersen and Sadaf Hosseini, 'Circular Water Solutions Key to Sustainable Data Centres', *World Economic Forum*, 7 November 2024, https://www.weforum.org/stories/2024/11/circular-water-solutions-sustainable-data-centres/

Tomašev, Nenad et al., 'AI for Social Good: Unlocking the Opportunity for Positive Impact', *Nature Communications*, 11 (2020), 2468, https://doi.org/10.1038/s41467-020-15871-z

United Nations, *Global E-Waste Monitor 2024*, https://ewastemonitor.info/

Wang, Peng, Ling-Yu Zhang, Asaf Tzachor and Wei-Qiang Chen, 'E-waste Challenges of Generative Artificial Intelligence', *Nat Comput Sci*, 4 (2024), 818–823, https://doi.org/10.1038/s43588-024-00712-6

United Nations Development Programme, *Sustainable Development Goals*, https://www.undp.org/africa/waca/sdgs-action

World Economic Forum, *AI for Impact: The PRISM Framework for Responsible AI in Social Innovation* (Geneva: WEF, 2024), https://www.weforum.org/publications/ai-for-impact-the-prism-framework-for-responsible-ai-in-social-innovation/

3. Security and AI: Holding the Line

John Magnus Furseth Kallevik

Only necessity is heavy, and only what is heavy has value.[1]

When we first explored this new digital continent of the internet, it was a lot like the Wild West. Doors stayed unlocked because danger was far away and sparse. Today the threat is on the doorstep, and sometimes already inside, carried in by ourselves in the form of IoT cameras, smart speakers, and 'helpful' sensors. We can still enjoy the ease of connected life, but only if we put weight where it matters: knowing what's in our house, who it answers to, and how to show it the door when it misbehaves.

Security is the weight we need so that value can exist. It is not just locks and passwords anymore; it is the integrity of the stories our systems tell. We built machines that answer, classify, deny and approve at machine speed. We trusted them because they were confident. But confidence is not truth, and speed is not safety.

Automation feels safe until it is not. A security dashboard full of green lights can hide a secret accidentally left in a log or an underlying AI model that changes results from one day to the next. When we cannot see or question the system, security turns into a feeling instead of a fact.

Consider an IT department that 'automates' incident response. Alerts flow into a model trained on last year's patterns. It suppresses what it thinks is noise, surfaces what it thinks is urgent. One day, a quiet anomaly dropped. The cybersecurity team never sees it. The breach is discovered weeks later by a student who notices strange logins on a shared lab PC. Responsibility stays human; authority drifts elsewhere. That gap is a real

1 Milan Kundera, *The Unbearable Lightness of Being*, trans. by Michael Henry Heim (New York: Harper & Row, 1984), p. 31.

 https://doi.org/10.11647/OBP.0530.03

security problem, just as it is a real problem for sovereignty.

There is another asymmetry we are only beginning to feel. These systems do not knock once and leave; they knock on every door, all the time. AI agents can probe, observe and learn patiently, twenty-four hours a day, building profiles not in minutes but over months. They do not guess at weak points; they discover them. Language, habits, response times, trust patterns, fatigue, all of it becomes a signal. When the pressure finally comes, it does not look like an attack. It looks like a perfectly timed message, a convincing request, a plausible instruction.

And somewhere down the line, a human pays for it. In time, in money, in reputation, or in trust. The machine never does. Markets may eventually punish unreliable systems, but only after the damage is done, and never on behalf of the people who paid the price first. IBM knew this in 1979: 'A computer can never be held accountable, therefore a computer must never make a management decision'.[2] The insight is half a century old. We are still learning to take it seriously.

The old mantra was 'trust but verify'. In AI, it must become 'verify before you trust'. That means knowing where the model runs and who can compel access. Jurisdiction is not just a footnote; it is often the weak link in the chain. When you prompt your enterprise language model through your local intranet, where does that prompt go? Through a myriad of networks and servers, to large language models running in data centres located far away in places few of us have ever heard of. To make matters even more complicated, a data centre on your own soil is not safe if someone else holds the keys or another country can knock. Even if we feel sovereign in our own jurisdiction, we need to follow the laws in the countries we want to conduct business in.

Verification means knowing what the model was trained on and whether your data is now part of someone else's prediction machine. It means knowing how the model fails, not just how it succeeds: inconsistent moderation, hallucinated facts, confident lies.

Weight, in security, is the discipline to slow down where it matters. Europe's take on safety is blunt: if a system can change your life, you must be able to push back; if something is synthetic, it should carry a

2 Doug Bonderud, 'AI Decision-making: Where Do Businesses Draw the Line?', *IBM*, https://www.ibm.com/think/insights/ai-decision-making-where-do-businesses-draw-the-line

label; reading emotions in intimate spaces is off-limits. Those rules do not live in a binder. They reshape what gets built, keeping humans in the loop and forcing transparency where power concentrates.

But law is not enough. Culture matters. We are quick to accept 'good enough' moderation, 'good enough' filters, 'good enough' privacy settings, until the day 'good enough' erases someone, labels someone or leaks someone. A glossy 'Protected by AI' banner means nothing if you cannot read the logs, cannot see how the model works, or lose control when another party asks for the data.

There is also a quiet erosion: calling everything 'just open data' and letting AI learn from it without consent. The EU's Digital Single Market framework carves out text and data mining limits for a reason. If AI becomes the memory of institutions, we need to decide whose stories it learns from and on what terms, instead of turning people's voices and creative works into features and skills for others to commercialize.

So what does weight look like in practice? Keep critical models and data where your own laws protect them. Not where another jurisdiction can reach in when it suits them. Build guardrails that are testable, not just documented. Does the model refuse what it should? Explain what it can? Log what it must? If you cannot answer those questions, you do not have security; you have the appearance of it. Decide which decisions must stay human, and hold that line even when speed is the argument for giving it up. And teach people to mistrust. Not as cynicism, but as competence. To ask who benefits from the shortcut. To recognise when 'protected by AI' is a marketing claim, not a guarantee.

Security does not have to be isolation. AI can help us defend faster, see patterns we miss, and automate the boring parts of protection. But we cannot let lightness, no matter how effortless, automatic or unexamined, become an excuse to forget how power moves.

A director of one of the largest cloud providers testified in France recently, under oath before the French Senate, that the company cannot guarantee data sovereignty against certain laws.[3] That is not a scandal;

3 Anton Carniaux, Director of Public and Legal Affairs, Microsoft France, testimony under oath before the French Senate inquiry on public procurement and digital sovereignty, 18 June 2025. Reported in: *The Register*, 'Microsoft Exec Admits It "Cannot Guarantee" Data Sovereignty', 25 July 2025, https://www.theregister.com/2025/07/25/microsoft_admits_it_cannot_guarantee

it is a reminder. Contracts and marketing pages promise lightness; jurisdiction and subpoenas deliver weight. If your incident response plan assumes your logs will always be yours, you have not planned for the day another country claims them.

I have long understood that what we put into computers becomes part of the record. Logs, messages, documents, tickets, alerts; all of it feels permanent, like entries in a history book we can return to when something goes wrong. What took me longer to fully grasp was who would own that history. Recording an event is not the same as controlling it. If your logs live in systems you cannot inspect, summarise or retrieve on your own terms, then your security history already belongs to someone else. And when incident records become training data, analytics or automated summaries outside your control, memory itself turns into an attack surface. Security is not only about preventing breaches; it is about ensuring that when something happens, you still own the story of what happened.

Security used to be framed as a technical discipline. Patch the server. Harden the code. Rotate the keys. All necessary. But the deeper work is choosing the weight you will accept. Weight is encryption you control. Weight is logging you can read. Weight is refusing to deploy a model that cannot be challenged, even if it boosts a metric. Weight is choosing a smaller, local model when the larger, remote one comes with a jurisdiction you do not trust. Open models you can run and inspect locally shift power from distant vendors to people who can own their stack.

Another uncomfortable truth is that exploits are hard to separate from learning itself. Prompt injection is often used to trick a model into ignoring its safeguards. A model cannot easily tell the difference between a sincere question, a clever reformulation, or a persistent attempt to bend its boundaries. If people are patient enough, or cruel enough, or simply curious enough, they will eventually find ways to coax unintended behaviour out of it. At the other end of the spectrum, injecting malicious prompts and data in training material can severely change the output of the model later, or even break training completely in extreme cases.

This is not hacking in the traditional sense; it is pressure applied through language. Social engineering against a social machine. We already see 'jailbreaks' and 'trick prompts' shared the way Google hacks once were, small incantations traded in forums and chats. As long as models learn from interaction, and as long as language remains flexible, no system is immune. Safety becomes probabilistic, not absolute. Sovereignty, then, cannot mean perfect control. It must mean knowing where failure is likely, who bears responsibility when it happens, and how quickly authority can be reclaimed when the magic breaks.

I remember when 'hacking' sometimes meant nothing more than knowing how to search. About 'Google hacks' where someone once put up a simple web page titled something like 'Hack Google', collecting clever queries that revealed what administrators had forgotten to lock down. Newly installed web servers often advertised themselves with demo pages, polite warnings that said, in effect, *please configure me*. Narrow that search to a specific software stack, then to a specific domain.

Narrow it further to government sites in a country you do not like, and suddenly you have a list of unsecured public servers in that region ready to own. No malware. No zero-days. Just patience and pattern recognition. Now amplify that with AI. Let agents scan continuously, correlate changes over time, track what appears, disappears, and reappears. What used to be a weekend curiosity becomes permanent reconnaissance. Security does not fail loudly here; it fails quietly, by being predictable.

Most institutions today are overwhelmed by the increase in spam, phishing attacks and network probing. Open-source software maintainers are drowning in code additions due to people vibe-coding with AI and submitting changes at levels we have not seen before. This makes it even harder to spot someone sending in malicious code to hope it slips under the radar. Manual control is not an option anymore. Vendors are using the mantra 'We need "Good AI" to stop "Bad AI"'. But this comes with its own risks.

Think about moderation. Different language models cannot agree on the same content. That inconsistency is a security risk. If your content filters depend on a model's mood, your enforcement is a lottery. If you cannot explain why a post was taken down or left up, you have built a black box of authority. And when people learn that the box is arbitrary, they will game it or ignore it. Either way, security fails.

The same 'lightness' lurks in synthetic content. A face that looks familiar. A voice that sounds right. A document that cites real things and invented things in the same breath. Deepfakes and machine-authored text do not need to be perfect to erode trust; they only need to be cheap and fast. Security is more than just locking your doors; you also need to know who is knocking before you open. We must mark synthetic content. Demand traceability. Weight is insisting on a chain of custody for digital reality.

Law helps. The EU's copyright framework draws lines around text and data mining; the AI Act draws lines around use of biometric and emotion analysis in sensitive spaces, and demands marking of synthetic content. These lines are imperfect, but they are weight. They say: this far, not further. They give practitioners a map. Ignore them, and you are not being innovative; you are being reckless with other people's autonomy.

Set explainability expectations. Not every decision needs a human-readable proof. But every decision that affects rights, access, or reputation must be contestable. If a model flags content as hate speech, there must be a path to understand why and to appeal. If a model downgrades a loan application, there must be a human accountable for that choice. If a model routes an incident away from human review, there must be evidence of how it made that call.

What about ethics? Too often 'ethics' is a fairness metric and a slide deck. Reviews of AI ethics practice show the gap between ambition and enforcement. Security has suffered the same fate: checklists without teeth. If your ethics review cannot veto a launch, it is theatre. If your security sign-off cannot stop a deployment, it is décor. Weight is giving these processes real power, even when it slows you down. Lightness is calling something 'secure' because a tool said so.

Remember my grandmother?[4] A small act of mistrust as a habit. That is the posture we need with AI. Use the tool, but keep your own mind awake. Verify the outputs. Compare across models. Demand explanations. Thinking that security is just another product you can buy is a dangerous route. As they say; "You cannot buy good taste ", this applies to security as well. Security is a posture you practice.

Cognitive warfare is already here. Bot farms can generate a thousand pages of mostly real news, with a little drop of their selected poison. Nobody reads this. But AI bots and models looking for training data

4 See Chapter 1 in this volume.

do. The poison spreads sideways, into training data, into the models that mediate our feeds and searches. In Norway and elsewhere, public debate about paying to train on trusted sources versus losing control to AI giants shows how live this risk is. The attack surface has expanded from our private perimeter to include the corpus of information that shapes what our systems think is true. Weight is curating training data, auditing sources and refusing to outsource truth to whoever shouts the loudest.

Public institutions feel this acutely. A government agency wants to use a language model to answer citizen questions. It is efficient. It is also a potential single point of failure. If the model invents a benefit that does not exist, who is accountable? If it quietly excludes people of certain dialects because it learned from skewed examples, who notices? If the logs live in a data centre subject to foreign laws, who can seize them? Security here is governance, transparency and the right to challenge.

At its core, security is about keeping choice in your own hands. That means using systems you can inspect, rules you can enforce and models you can test. AI will tempt us to stop looking. To let the model decide. To let the vendor assure. To let the dashboard soothe. We need to resist that. Keep the habit of looking. Keep the habit of asking. Keep the habit of saying no.

After all, even the most powerful supercomputers we have these days are still struggling to predict the weather, but our grandparents always knew when a storm was coming. Use your instincts.

Memory matters because forgetting lets power repeat itself. We should keep records of incidents, near-misses and abuses, not out of fear for the future, but to learn from the past. AI gives us an unprecedented ability to analyze vast amounts of data, this should be used to learn, not to surveil; to see where controls failed, rather than looking for a scapegoat to blame. Weight is institutional memory that informs design, lightness is knowing that your data is safe in the hands of their caretakers.

AI can help defend, spot odd patterns, block bad links, catch malware faster. Machines can learn our patterns to look for the anomaly our human eyes would not catch. But each gain must come with an honest accounting of loss: explainability, jurisdictional risk, data spill, model drift.

We can be light enough to adapt and heavy enough to be accountable. That is the balance.

AI DISCLAIMER: In the writing of this chapter, the author has used AI tools for organization of information and research, and for analysis of text and feedback. The written text is his own and not AI-generated.

References

Bonderud, Doug, 'AI Decision-making: Where Do Businesses Draw the Line?', *IBM*, https://www.ibm.com/think/insights/ai-decision-making-where-do-businesses-draw-the-line

Kundera, Milan, *The Unbearable Lightness of Being*, trans. by Michael Henry Heim (New York: Harper & Row, 1984).

Kunert, Paul, 'Microsoft Exec Admits It "Cannot Guarantee" Data Sovereignty', *The Register*, 25 July 2025, https://www.theregister.com/2025/07/25/microsoft_admits_it_cannot_guarantee

4. Governing AI in Complex Organisations: Why Sustainability and Inclusion are Key Success Factors

Simon Whittemore and Giuliano Pozza

Purpose, Values and Organisational Culture

To understand the impact of AI on organisations, we need first to establish what defines organisations regardless of AI, to avoid the danger of implicit assumptions distorting the debate. Organisations, including businesses of all types, are part of society. The economic context in which they operate is also part of society, not a parallel universe with its own rules and regulations. Businesses, therefore, exist to serve society. Every business depends on the quality of its relationships with employees, customers, suppliers and wider society.

This may seem the heavy side of being rather than the lightness, but it is bearable because with the 'heaviness' comes meaning, purpose and, ultimately, fulfilment. According to the Blueprint for Better Business, 'business is society's most effective vehicle to bring people and resources together to create value'.[1] Governance ensures accountability so that the organisation stays true to its declared purpose, values, commitments and responsibilities in creating shared value. In a later section of this

1 Blueprint for Business, *The Purpose of Purpose*, https://www.blueprintforbusiness.org/the-purpose-of-purpose/

 https://doi.org/10.11647/OBP.0530.04

chapter, we investigate the impact of AI on governance.

AI, when adopted broadly across the organisation, can call into question both purpose and values. For example, a university that encourages the widespread use of a powerful generative AI tool by students and staff without due governance, may find students questioning the educational purpose of its courses or the institution.[2] Purpose (encapsulated in the mission) is why the organisation exists and how society benefits from its existence, and serves to 'move people to commit to a shared worthwhile endeavour'.[3]

Core values, guiding principles communicated both internally and externally, shape how the purpose is fulfilled. Does AI challenge or fit within these core organisational values? The values espoused are not always the 'lived' values; if the leaders of an organisation do not act as role models or if they perpetuate behaviours that contradict or demean the declared values—for example, at Enron where a core espoused value was integrity—then the values are empty of meaning, and the organisation is unlikely to be either authentic or trustworthy.[4] Organisations need to ensure they 'walk the talk' when it comes to values so they are genuinely reflected in their culture, according to employees' lived experience. Of course, core values are not set in stone, but even if reviewed and updated, to be credible, they still need to reflect stakeholders' lived experience rather than be empty claims.

AI may present a challenge or an opportunity for the espoused values. For example, if sustainability is a core value, then indiscriminate use of the most powerful large language models undermines this value, since the data centres that power AI consume vast amounts of energy and water, leaving a carbon footprint comparable to that of a global city such as New York, according to research at Vrije Universiteit Amsterdam.[5] A

2 Aisha Down, '"We could have asked ChatGPT": Students Fight Back Over Course Taught by AI', *The Guardian*, 20 November 2025, https://www.theguardian.com/education/2025/nov/20/university-of-staffordshire-course-taught-in-large-part-by-ai-artificial-intelligence

3 Blueprint for Business, *The Purpose of Purpose*, https://www.blueprintforbusiness.org/the-purpose-of-purpose/

4 P. Arvind, 'Integrity Lost: The Stunning Collapse of Enron's Empire', *AP Thinks*, 15 August 2025, https://apthinks.com/integrity-lost-the-stunning-collapse-of-enrons-empire/

5 Alex de Vries-Gao, 'The Carbon and Water Footprints of Data Centers and What This Could Mean for Artificial Intelligence', *Patterns*, 7.1 (2025), 101430, https://doi.

2026 analysis by Ketan Joshi and six global sustainability organisations also found that claims that AI delivers climate benefit were misleading and largely unsubstantiated, in that the benefits claimed (mainly in corporate websites rather than academic papers) related to 'traditional AI' ('narrow' machine learning),[6] rather than to consumer generative AI, which has a much greater negative impact on the climate (see the above cited Dutch research). Nevertheless, the potential of machine learning through climate analytics is widely recognised. Equally, if inclusion is one of the people-related values, then this may be challenged by the fact that AI systems used are likely to have been trained on culturally and socially biased data (though on the other side of the coin, AI can also bring exciting new possibilities for inclusion, as explored in Chapter 9 in this volume). On the positive side, a core value such as innovation can be enhanced by the carefully governed application of AI to specific problems, such as responding to a vast number of similar enquiries or analysing complex and dynamic information for patterns; this can deliver significant benefits not only for the organisation's efficiency, but also for its knowledge and data management.

Core values, if embedded and enacted, reflect the culture of an organisation. Ownership and accountability are often cited as core values, typically together with results-orientation. This perhaps represents the greatest challenge to organisations that adopt generative AI extensively; there is mounting evidence to suggest that frequent interaction with generative AI can directly alter the sense of agency and responsibility in users, resulting in the outsourcing of accountability.[7] This poses potentially serious risks for organisations and individual users, 'outsourcing' core elements of individual and organisational learning, pulling the behavioural culture away from a learning culture to a transactional one.

On the other hand, collaboration, which was the most common core value in a sample of UK companies, could be enriched by AI

---

org/10.1016/j.patter.2025.101430

6 Joshi, Ketan, *The AI Climate Hoax: Behind the Curtain of How Big Tech Greenwashes Impacts* (Berlin: Beyond Fossil Fuels, 2026), https://beyondfossilfuels.org/wp-content/uploads/2026/02/AI-for-climate-claims-Report_FEB-2026_FINAL-2-16.pdf

7 Adriana Salatino, Arthur Prével, Emilie Caspar and Salvatore Lo Bue, 'Influence of AI Behavior on Human Moral Decisions, Agency, and Responsibility', *Scientific Reports*, 15 (2025), Article 95587, https://doi.org/10.1038/s41598-025-95587-6

and specifically through collaboration with AI, in new and creative dynamics, without losing the human agency.[8] There is much promise in the potential for harnessing the power of AI in creating collaborative capital by carefully integrating the former, in the service, for example, of community engagement so that it reinforces, rather than undermines, shared organisational purpose.[9]

To ensure that embracing AI does not jeopardise the strategic anchoring of purpose, mission and values, organisations need to ask themselves again the same questions posed in the strategic development process. They are critical questions for leadership, but also for all who use AI systems substantially, so should ideally be addressed as part of an open strategy process.[10] These questions include who do the new systems serve; what constitutes organisational knowledge and whose knowledge counts; how authority and accountability is exercised through the use of the new systems and how is their use governed; which assumptions (e.g. purpose, values) are treated as non-negotiable.

If organisations integrate AI deeply and broadly without asking these questions, then there is a risk that in rushing to implement AI for competitive gain, they may find themselves guided by AI, rather than guided by their own purpose, governance and strategy. And while that may feel initially like a lightness of being, the organisational cultural 'edifice' will be at the mercy of high winds, and indeed strategic drift, without the shared foundation of purpose and the cornerstones of core values and good governance.

A Governance Framework

Governance frameworks are invaluable instruments to assure coherence between purpose, strategy, goals and outcomes and to avoid the undesirable aforementioned effects. To walk the talk, organisations need

8 University of Oxford, 'The Most Prominent UK Business Values Do Not Include Humility or Gratitude—Oxford Study', *University of Oxford*, 4 August 2022, https://www.ox.ac.uk/news/2022-08-04-most-prominent-uk-business-values-do-not-include-humility-or-gratitude-oxford-study

9 Cassandra Overney, 'Designing for Constructive Civic Communication: A Framework for Human-AI Collaboration in Community Engagement Processes', *arXiv* preprint, 16 May 2025, https://doi.org/10.48550/arXiv.2505.11684

10 Julia Hautz, David Seidl and Richard Whittington, 'Open Strategy: Dimensions, Dilemmas, Dynamics', *Long Range Planning*, 50.3 (2017), 298–309, https://doi.org/10.1016/j.lrp.2016.12.001

a clear structure of roles, responsibilities and governance processes specifically focused on AI so to align intentions and execution.

In the literature, there are quite a number of proposals for AI governance frameworks.[11] Many of them are focused on providing guidelines on how to address AI at a regulatory or risk management level. Two examples of these kinds of frameworks are the European Union's AI Act (EU AI Act)[12] and the National Institute of Standards and Technology's AI Risk Management Framework (NIST AI RMF).[13]

However, to frame our discussion we will use a more comprehensive approach, inspired partially by ISACA's Governance of Enterprise IT and partially by ISO 42001, the first international standard for an Artificial Intelligence Management System (AIMS).[14] We mixed a specific AI framework with a more general one for two reasons: first and foremost, a governance framework should include all the aspects of governance, not only management: strategy definition, value management and resource considerations are at least as important as risk. Second, at its core, governance is about defining roles, responsibilities and processes that align strategic goals with execution in techno-human organisations. Since humans have not changed much with the advent of AI (at least so far, see Chapter 10 in this volume for a glance of what the future might look like), we can assume that the good practices in governance hold true also for AI. And even if AI does present an uncharted kind of novelty compared with other innovations, it is nevertheless a digital technology that must be interpreted in connection with other digital technologies.

Following the comprehensive approach proposed, we will articulate our discussion in four domains:

- Strategic Management;
- Resource Optimisation;
- Risk Optimisation;
- Benefits Realisation.

11 Amna Batool, Didar Zowghi and Muneera Bano, 'AI Governance: A Systematic Literature Review', *arXiv* preprint, 24 July 2024, https://doi.org/10.48550/arXiv.2401.10896

12 See https://artificialintelligenceact.eu/

13 See https://www.nist.gov/itl/ai-risk-management-framework

14 See https://www.iso.org/standard/42001

However, discussing each domain level, we will highlight a number of differences from traditional governance models and we will try to focus in our discussion on the aspects of the domains more relevant to AI, including the implications for inclusion and sustainability. One last note: we will need to slightly stretch the traditional concept of 'IT governance' to include the governance of operational technologies (OTs)[15] as well. It is probably useful to remember that digital technologies rest on two pillars: information technologies (all the devices and applications used to manage data and information) and operational technologies (all systems and devices that operate on the physical environment to monitor and control devices, processes and events). Agentic AI,[16] a breed of AI system that is fully or partially autonomous in setting and pursuing a goal, promises to become one of the most powerful OTs invented so far, though it remains in an experimental phase right now.

First Domain: Strategic Management

A famous aphorism, credited to the Roman philosopher Seneca, states: 'There is no favourable wind for the sailor who doesn't know where to go'.[17] The motto holds true for AI as well. Looking at the status of AI implementations in many organisations, it seems that the wind is strong and growing, but the strategic direction of the organisations is uncertain. The truth is that seldom has a clear AI strategy been defined, since experimenting and piloting AI projects (what most organisations are doing right now) can hardly be considered a strategy, and a full-blown governance model is a rarity. Defining an AI strategy, coordinated with the overall digital strategy and backed up by a sound governance framework, is essential to assure that strategy execution will be aligned with the strategic vision. What is peculiar to AI, as for many other radical innovations, is that the context, the opportunities and the risks

15 You can find the NIST definition of OT here: https://csrc.nist.gov/glossary/term/operational_technology

16 For a definition, see Beth Stackpole, 'Agentic AI, Explained', *MIT Management*, 18 February 2026, https://mitsloan.mit.edu/ideas-made-to-matter/agentic-ai-explained

17 Lucius Annaeus Seneca, *Epistulae Morales ad Lucilium* (Letters to Lucilius), Letter 71 (commonly translated as 'If a man does not know to which port he sails, no wind is favourable').

are continuously changing. So, the cycles to plan, implement, evaluate and review the strategy should be short and iterative. And pivoting (i.e. redefining and sometimes radically changing the strategy) is an ever-present option. The paradigm is closer to lean start-up[18] than to traditional IT governance.

Once the strategic vision is defined, the next problem is to assure alignment between strategy and execution. The alignment problem is more general than IT governance, as Harari has well expressed in *Nexus*,[19] but is more complicated in a fast-changing context. Here a number of classical governance tools can help, from the responsibility assignment matrix RACI (which stands for Responsible, Accountable, Consulted and Informed) or the RACIVS matrix (Responsible, Accountable, Consulted, Informed, Verifies, Signs-Off) to Agile best practices. In many organisations, an AI committee, distinct from the IT committee or digital committee, is deemed necessary in order to maintain the necessary agility and focus. The key point here is that the top management of the organisation, including the board, should be involved both in strategy definition and in governance of AI. The implications are so vast that it cannot be delegated. And, to avoid common mistakes that many organisations are making right now, here are a few suggestions to be considered when developing an AI strategy and AI governance model.

First of all, do not focus on information technology only. The NIS2 Directive[20] makes it clear that OTs, as defined earlier, are just as important as IT in the context of cybersecurity. And for AI, OT systems will effectively become the agents driving the next wave of disruption. It is paramount to agree on a strategy for agent definition and management, but also a strategy for agent orchestration. What architecture and what technologies/partners does the organisation plan to use? What are the roles and responsibilities of the different actors, humans and synthetic?

Secondly, if an organisation does not plan for inclusion and sustainability from the very inception of its strategy, it is jeopardising its AI journey. In fact, a non-inclusive AI programme will reap only a portion of the potential benefits for employees and customers/client,

18 To learn more, start from here: https://theleanstartup.com/

19 Yuval Noah Harari, *Nexus: A Brief History of Information Networks from the Stone Age to AI* (London: Fern Press, 2024).

20 See https://digital-strategy.ec.europa.eu/en/policies/nis2-directive

exposing an organisation to reputational and other risks. Not only can sustainability, or the lack thereof, be a reputational risk, but more concretely, the IT budget will soon get out of control. A well-defined strategy will include considerations about architecture, environmental impacts, social effects and cost structure of your services.

Third, it is important not to forget the enablers for an effective strategy and governance: principles/policies, processes, organisational structures, culture/ethics, people, skills and competences. We will explore some of these enablers in the next sections.

Last but not least, the data and knowledge base (KB) set-up and governance should receive a special focus. AI is similar to business intelligence in this respect. The outcome is simply as good as the raw materials (data, knowledge base articles, and so on) used to feed the machine. And building and maintaining a quality KB can be a daunting task at a minimum. Remember that while AI can do much for our organisations, before AI starts working for us... we need to work for AI. Again, better planning for it in advance and making data and KB governance a structural part of any organisation strategy.

Second Domain: Resource Optimisation

AI is resource hungry. The impact on budgets, human resources and sustainability for organisations responding to the 'AI rush' is substantial, with evident costs and often unclear benefits.[21] Taking a strategic resource-based view (RBV),[22] as first proposed by Edith Penrose (1959),[23] the question is: can AI enhance and enrich organisational resources, whether these are 'tangible' resources such as facilities, finance and the IT estate, or intangible resources, such as competencies, efficiency and innovation. Case studies and analysis suggest that in both areas AI can offer value, especially by developing capabilities and organisational learning.[24] There

---

21 Alexander Golev, 'Microsoft 365 Copilot Licensing Guide: Costs and ROI', *SAMexpert*, 2 December 2025, https://samexpert.com/microsoft-365-copilot-licensing/

22 See https://www.futurelearn.com/info/courses/introduction-to-international-human-resources-management/0/steps/95993

23 E. T. Penrose, *The Theory of the Growth of the Firm* (New York: John Wiley, 1959).

24 Paavo Ritala, Päivi Aaltonen, Mika Ruokonen and Andre Nemeh, 'Developing Industrial AI Capabilities: An Organisational Learning Perspective', *Technovation*, 138 (2024), 103120, https://doi.org/10.1016/j.technovation.2024.103120

are some significant caveats in both areas that currently indicate the impact of AI is, on balance, a weight rather than a lightness, as AI is heavy on resources, especially budget.

A task-based (matrix) rather than person- or role-based (temple) organisational culture,[25] combined with a skills-based rather than role-based workforce strategy, constitute a key strategic basis for managing and benefiting from AI sustainably and inclusively. AI will have an impact on virtually all roles, so the ability to develop flexibility, adaptability and learning agility in staff within the strategic objective of being a learning organisation is vital. This will involve some training but more important will be learning by doing and through collaboration, whether in pilot projects or in developing the foundational capabilities outlined below.

Facing the rapid change, market disruption and opportunities presented by AI, organisations with critical mass and investment ability would benefit from adopting a strategic approach that prioritises dynamic capabilities,[26] as this is a proven method for adapting one's resources in a context of rapid technological change. In practice, this involves developing the strategic ability to reconfigure key organisational capabilities, such as knowledge management and cross-functional collaboration. In the early 2000s, Apple and Samsung, through sensing (scanning for opportunities), seizing (choosing and addressing them) and reconfiguring (adapting organisational capabilities) exploited opportunities that Motorola, Nokia and Ericsson were not able or willing to exploit. However, with AI, the stakes are higher and reconfiguring organisational resources around the main offers of one or two leading brands such as OpenAI or Anthropic is loaded with risk, especially given that the former, and to a lesser extent the latter, are nowhere near breaking even economically.[27] Therefore, the theme of resource optimisation and AI is

25 See C. Handy, *Understanding Organizations*, 4th edition (Harmondsworth: Penguin), p. 185.

26 D. Teece and G. Pisano, 'The Dynamic Capabilities of Firms: An Introduction', *Industrial and Corporate Change*, 3 (1994), 537–556, https://doi.org/10.1093/icc/3.3.537-a

27 Abhinav, 'The Cost of Intelligence: AI Future Is Unsustainable in its Current Form of Growth', *Medium*, 22 October 2025, https://medium.com/@abhinav0231/the-cost-of-intelligence-e55827c7bfeb. Direct X, 'OpenAI: The Billion-Dollar Burn—Will It Ever Be Profitable?', *Medium*, 4 November 2025, https://medium.com/%40directX/

not so much about brands as about internal strategic and operational capability. When we consider the dynamic capabilities approach to AI, we should bear in mind that there are two distinct strategic aspects, each with different, but mutually dependent capabilities required.

One aspect is developing the AI capabilities themselves, which requires the organisation to have the innovation processes, learning agility, technical competencies, databases and budget to be able to offer new and distinctive or market-changing AI-generated opportunities, directly or indirectly. The other concerns developing the capabilities to integrate, manage and govern AI, so that the organisation manages the risks, creates a coherent strategy to interpret, position and address AI advancements. The former is where the dynamic capabilities approach will pay dividends, but arguably they are two sides of the same coin, since you cannot achieve the former sustainably and securely, without mastering the latter.

Foundational Capabilities

Seen in this light, it becomes clear that there are certain threshold capabilities for organisations that wish to integrate and benefit from AI; capabilities that are essential foundations to be able to function in the AI context. AI, like every major technology advance, requires investment, but the good news is that this investment in capabilities will pay off for businesses in a myriad of other ways, including as a vital prerequisite for the next major technology advance, quantum computing. So, while AI itself can drain budget and other resources, managing and improving the foundational capabilities highlighted below is a sound investment, which should be considered part of the overall cost-benefits business case for AI.

What are these 'foundational capabilities'? Deploying AI effectively requires a high level of data integrity, accuracy and completeness, and technical debt must be properly managed and minimised. This work to improve databases, manage technical debt (without over-reliance on new cloud-based systems) and govern and manage data more effectively can only benefit the organisation in the process of 'knowing itself' well. Indeed, both for individuals and organisations, strong and

---

openai-the-billion-dollar-burn-will-it-ever-be-profitable-536be8c90251

clear self-knowledge is critical before engaging with AI; individuals can undermine their personal identity all too easily with indiscriminate use of generative AI,[28] just as organisations can compromise their identity management and their data security without robust AI governance.[29]

There are also some essential core skills that staff need in organisations integrating AI. It is no secret that AI adoption calls for an enhanced focus on and development of 'soft skills'. These transversal competencies, to use a more meaningful term, matter more than ever in the age of AI.[30] Together with self-knowledge, foremost among these is learning agility: to be able to learn efficiently from experience and apply the lessons learnt in different and changing contexts.[31] This is a uniquely human skill in that learning efficiently (from minimal data and signals, as, in fact, a baby does) contrasts with machine learning and LLMs, which require vast information resources to detect patterns and thus generate useful and plausible content. Learning agility can be enhanced by doing, but it needs to be recognised and supported by the leadership and HR.

Another vital transversal competency for organisational adopting AI is critical and independent thinking.[32] It is well documented that the uncritical adoption of generative AI can damage critical thinking both in individuals and organisations.[33] Solutions that offer unprecedented levels of convenience and can deliver answers and results to complex queries in seconds are seductive, just as popular online search engines are, giving the sense that you can have the world's knowledge at your fingertips, despite advertising and SEO-driven results. Here, the concept of media

---

28 Lawrence R. Samuel, 'Is Artificial Intelligence a Threat to Personal Identity?', *Psychology Today*, 17 December 2025, https://www.psychologytoday.com/gb/blog/psychology-yesterday/202512/is-artificial-intelligence-a-threat-to-personal-identity

29 Sepideh Rowland, 'The Identity Dilemma: How AI Blurs the Line Between Reality and Fraud', *The Financial Brand*, 2 January 2026, https://thefinancialbrand.com/news/banking-technology/ai-id-fraud-bank-194966

30 Moh Hosseinioun, Frank Neffke, Hyejin Youn and Letian (LT) Zhang, 'Soft Skills Matter Now More Than Ever, According to New Research', *Harvard Business Review*, 26 August 2025, https://hbr.org/2025/08/soft-skills-matter-now-more-than-ever-according-to-new-research

31 Simon Whittemore, 'Transversal Competencies for Sustainable Employability — An Overview and a Vade Mecum' (white paper, May 2023), p. 63.

32 Ibid., p. 65.

33 Olivia Guest, Marcela Suarez, Barbara Müller et al., 'Against the Uncritical Adoption of "AI" Technologies in Academia', position paper, 13 September 2025, https://doi.org/10.5281/zenodo.17065099

and information literacy applied to the digital world is even more vital for AI, as part of the necessary critical thinking. It is all too easy to ask AI and receive 'the answer'. Organisations need to actively develop and improve critical and independent thinking in employees and all stakeholders to avoid misleading assumptions and poor decision-making.

Collaboration and boundary-spanning skills are also foundational competencies for AI integration. Workers will of course need to collaborate effectively with colleagues in a range of different roles, and across organisational and functional boundaries and silos, to integrate and manage AI, but they will also need to collaborate with AI itself, which will require targeted training and development, learning how to use AI as a co-design partner, while keeping the human hands on the reins. It is in this process of developing collaborative capital that businesses can achieve significant progress as learning organisations.

Here, we have concentrated deliberately on the foundational capabilities for AI (governance is dealt with in the preceding section), but clearly there are some new AI technical capabilities without which organisations will struggle to capitalise on the opportunities. Any generative AI agent or interface requires precise instructions ('prompting' is the term used at the time of writing) and to get the best results, these often need to be quite detailed and structured, including stating the context, examples, limitations and role, if relevant. This is therefore a core skill for using generative AI effectively which requires practice, so some training is a sound investment, as it is with regard to the critical evaluation of outputs highlighted above. In addition, the new capabilities and roles emerging include data governance experts, AI ethics leads and AI orchestrators (multimodal AI and suites of LLMs). Some in-house AI legal expertise will also be required; this is a fast-changing field in which case law is emergent, the incipient legal framework is shifting and the technology is advancing rapidly.

Just as challenges offer learning and personal development opportunities for individuals, the advent of AI can offer opportunities for organisational development. Governing and integrating AI effectively enhances agile learning across the organisation and requires tighter data controls, optimised data resources and an adaptable, stimulated and collaborative workforce. This may sound like heavy work, as building foundations are, but such discipline will pay dividends and enable the selected AI tools to bring value to a stable base with a relatively light touch.

Third Domain: Risk Management

With the rise of AI, risk management received a strong focus and there are several frameworks addressing the topic. While we do not undertake a systematic literature review in this section, the aforementioned European Union's AI Act (EU AI Act) and the US National Institute of Standards and Technology's AI Risk Management Framework (NIST AI RMF) remain essential reference points. They can be thought of as complementary: EU's AI Act explains what should be done to properly manage AI risk, while NIST AI RMF offers a practical model showing how to manage risk. While we do not explore these frameworks further, they underscore the importance of AI risk management for advancing inclusion and sustainability.

Inclusion is crucial in risk management not only for ethical or utilitarian reasons (avoiding brand reputation risks, for example). It is more than that. Inclusion avoids groupthink, a term coined by William Whyte and developed by Irving Janis to describe the 'tendency for groups to become so concerned about group solidarity that they fail to critically and realistically evaluate their decisions, initial viewpoints, and assumptions'.[34] Inclusion improves decision-making, helping to build a more resilient culture by harnessing the richness of diverse viewpoints and backgrounds. In such a highly challenging and highly volatile context as AI, leaving out even just one of your employees or clients/customers could be both an unacceptable risk and a lost opportunity.

The same focus should be applied in risk management to sustainability as well: the risk of introducing in an organisation a technology that is not sustainable is unacceptable. And for organisations, as for society at large, the sustainability risks should be addressed at the economic, social and environmental levels

Our recommendation here is to verify that, whatever risk management framework your organisation will choose, inclusion and sustainability risks should be properly addressed.

One final remark about agentic AI: it is an example of OT with unprecedented power. This in turn means that agents pose an unprecedented level of risk, due to the following possibilities:

---

34 F. R. C. de Wit, 'The Paradox of Intragroup Conflict', PhD dissertation, Kurt Lewin Instituut, 2013, https://hdl.handle.net/1887/20566, pp. 10-11.

- **Destructive or unauthorised actions:** agents can perform destructive actions affecting real work; they do not just generate generic outputs for human evaluation. This can constitute both a security and a safety risk.
- **Command misinterpretation:** commands that appear legitimate can be interpreted in harmful ways, especially when the context is unusual, extreme or poorly specified.
- **Adversarial manipulation:** agents can be manipulated by external attackers with serious effects, for example via prompt injection.[35]

A few agentic-specific risk management frameworks are emerging: the most notable are the Agent Risk Capability framework by the Singapore Government and Agentic AI by the Open Worldwide Application Security Project. They can be used in conjunction with other frameworks, like NIST AI RMF, which is more general but less specific about agents.

Fourth Domain: Benefits Realisation

A sobering MIT report in July 2025, researching over 300 AI initiatives, found that 95% of companies surveyed have not been able to produce value with AI.[36] This is despite widespread adoption and a global investment in AI of 252 billion US dollars in 2024.[37] This reality contrasts starkly with the vast number of hyperbolic projections by the AI industry and management consultancies, such as the McKinsey claim that AI could boost productivity by $4 trillion annually.[38]

The point here is not so much whether AI will deliver benefits; clearly

35 Prompt injection is a security vulnerability where attackers bypass an AI model's safety guardrails or instructions by embedding malicious commands within user input or external data.

36 Aditya Challapally, Chris Pease, Ramesh Raskar and Pradyumna Chari, *The GenAI Divide: State of AI in Business 2025* (Project NANDA, 2025), https://mlq.ai/media/quarterly_decks/v0.1_State_of_AI_in_Business_2025_Report.pdf

37 Njenga Kariuki, 'Economy', in N. Maslej, L. Fattorini, R. Perrault et al., *Artificial Intelligence Index Report 2025* (Stanford, CA: Stanford Institute for Human-Centered AI, 2025), https://hai.stanford.edu/ai-index/2025-ai-index-report/economy

38 McKinsey and Company, 'The Economic Potential of Generative AI: The Next Productivity Frontier', 14 June 2023, https://www.mckinsey.com/capabilities/tech-and-ai/our-insights/the-economic-potential-of-generative-ai-the-next-productivity-frontier

it will, and is already showing promise, notably as machine learning applied to specific issues such as climate prediction or detecting patterns across large datasets in the legal and medical fields.[39] Rather, we need to recognise that part and parcel of AI is the hype and the propaganda that goes with it, especially generative AI. Financial returns and profitability are obviously not the only indicators of success; many technologies such as the internet itself as invented by Tim Berners-Lee and colleagues at CERN, were established and initially utilised to deliver public value and access to information to citizens rather than profits, but they were not driven by billions of dollars of financial speculation and marketing.

Even MIT itself had to retract a paper which was full of inflated benefits predictions for a range of sectors. In the new climate of relative realism, some scaling back and disinvestment is inevitable. This private sector realism has triggered a new focus on thinly spread public sector provision, where valuable services (e.g. UK Citizens Advice Bureau) could be replaced by AI and thus generate significant savings to keep AI afloat.

The above findings are mainly concerned with the potential financial benefits of AI such as investment, revenue or savings, but clearly, we should look for value elsewhere too. The section on resources above highlights how organisations can use the AI opportunity to improve their 'foundational capabilities', such as data security and integrity, collaboration and learning agility. These are real benefits catalysed by AI. What of other key organisational goods, such as inclusion and sustainability; does AI contribute to value in these areas? Both topics are dealt with separately in earlier chapters, so here we will limit ourselves to noting that AI brings both benefits and threats to inclusion and threats and benefits to sustainability; the order of these words is deliberate.

As digital technologies have done for some time, AI offers new and exciting possibilities in the area of inclusion and equality. All the caveats expressed previously in this chapter apply, in particular that to bring these opportunities to fruition, we need to recognise that a) AI tools may be natively biased due to their training and specific cultural origins and b) we need to work with AI, with due diligence, before it works for us. One striking example of how AI can be used to enhance inclusion, as

39 See further https://www.adaptation-fund.org/wp-content/uploads/2025/03/Scoping-Study-on-Use-of-AI-in-Evaluations-03.24.25v2.pdf

well as journalistic standards and constructive engagement, is that of the *Financial Times*. The *FT* developed an automated comment moderation solution, trained on a large sample of reader comments, which filters out racist and sexist comments and offensive language in line with their editorial policy as a responsible publisher and mindful of UK hate crime laws, yet encourages constructive, stimulating feedback and debate.[40] There is no question of this curtailing free speech in the UK, as in the UK the latter is protected in the Human Rights Act which incorporates the European Convention on Human Rights, and is nevertheless balanced by the Public Order Act and Online Safety Act. This is an inspiring example of how the power of AI can be deployed to support and strengthen democracy, especially since the comments section is a major dilemma for most news and features outlets.

Sustainability is a greater challenge, since many of the major LLMs have been developed with socially unsustainable and exploitative practices, including scraping the internet of content, regardless of whether it is in the public domain or not.[41] Then, of course, there is the enormous and rapidly growing energy consumption and carbon footprint of AI. AI is not only an extremely data-hungry form of advanced computing but also, it has been calculated, consumes as much water as the entire global consumption of bottled water.[42]

Without understating the negative impact of AI, however, we should also emphasise that AI can make an enormous contribution to sustainability in a variety of sectors.[43] Through largescale, multimodal data analysis, pattern recognition and predictive modelling, AI, in particular, applied as machine learning rather than generative AI, is a powerful ally in climate analytics, monitoring deforestation and reducing waste in urban planning and farming, for example.[44] There are

---

40 Anna Bruno, 'How Artificial Intelligence Helps the *Financial Times* to Moderate the Comments', *annabruno.it* (n.d.), https://www.annabruno.it/en/as-artificial-lintellimation-helps-the-financial-times-to-moderate-the-comments/

41 'AI & IP: Addressing the Challenges of Data Scraping and the OECD View', *IP Solved*, 19 February 2025, https://ipsolved.com/news/posts/ai-ip-addressing-the-challenges-of-data-scraping-and-the-oecd-view/

42 de Vries-Gao, 'The Carbon and Water Footprints of Data Centers'.

43 Lipika Bhattacharya, 'Why AI's Role in Advancing Sustainability is Underestimated', *World Economic Forum*, 3 March 2025, https://www.weforum.org/stories/2025/03/can-ai-foster-sustainability/

44 W. Y. Leong, 'Artificial Intelligence-Driven Analytics for Monitoring and Mitigating Climate Change Impacts', *Engineering Proceedings*, 108 (2025) 7, https://doi.

opportunities for organisations to contribute to these initiatives and help make AI a force for good, while minimising the organisational footprint. For a more detailed discussion, see Chapter 2 in this volume.

We started by examining the question of AI return on investment, but a more nuanced lens through which to examine AI benefits is via stakeholders, from employees to customers. AI brings opportunities that require collaboration, both with colleagues and with the AI tools themselves. Employees can benefit from AI through collaborative working models, continuous learning in hybrid teams and shared innovation opportunities. Constructive managed engagement with AI tends to break down silos as it requires separate departments and functions to interact in new and productive ways. If carefully and sensitively harnessed, AI can thereby enhance organisations' collaborative capital and advance the journey towards being a learning organisation, developing and cross-pollinating new skills, both transversal and technical.

The productivity and efficiency enhancement credentials of AI represent a solid opportunity for organisations to realise benefits and, at the same time, liberate staff to concentrate on more value-creating and strategic tasks. Repetitive, time-consuming tasks which have little variability, such as managing predictable enquiry flows or dealing with feedback can be automated via trained AI virtual assistants, which are becoming more sophisticated with sentiment and preference analysis and can enhance the customer interface.

The disappointing returns on AI highlighted at the beginning of this section are due in part to overambitious and unrealistic predictions, and in part to an underestimation of how much work is required in organisations to integrate AI effectively and safely into established processes and to create and maintain the high-quality databases on which AI depends. There are already many examples and case studies demonstrating how AI can help to better inform decision-making, enhance efficiency and stimulate innovation. Importantly, in strategy analysis, AI can provide the organisation with far greater precision in predictive analytics, and therefore make strategic development activities, including scenario planning and horizon scanning, far more effective.[45]

org/10.3390/engproc2025108007

45 'The Role of AI in Business Strategies for 2025 and Beyond', *The Strategy Institute*,

Nevertheless, all things considered, we should perhaps just accept that we are still in the infancy of AI and the journey to the productive use of this powerful advanced technology is only just beginning.

Conclusions: An Adventurous Journey

> Adventures? Nasty, disturbing, uncomfortable things! Make you late for dinner! I don't know what any of you see in them.[46]

We close this chapter quoting Bilbo Baggins once again, as in the introduction. It is indeed an adventurous journey that we are undertaking with AI. And we have no idea what is coming next! According to many observers, the AI bubble is about to burst.[47] The views of a relative insider, close to the tech industry, are particularly illuminating. Michael Burry, the US trader who famously and correctly predicted the 2008 sub-prime crash, has recently opined that the AI boom is a 'glorious folly'.[48] He has already taken steps to disinvest profitably from Nvidia and Palantir, the two major tech companies that underpin much of AI, and that are currently valued in inflated terms.

What will be the impact on organisations if and when the AI bubble bursts? Well, there will still be AI, as it is already being integrated, providing new insights and stimulating innovation. There was the dotcom bubble, but digital tools still transformed organisations globally. AI might be less freely accessible, but that is no bad thing as this will give organisations more control and precision in their cost/benefit analysis. When the inflated bubble bursts, we can then focus better on AI for good, AI for all and AI in the service of sustainability and inclusion: a much lighter and more bearable burden for organisations.

So, we are back again to the archetype of the struggle between weight and lightness. It is an omnipresent theme with AI, two forces that are

---

13 January 2025, https://www.thestrategyinstitute.org/insights/the-role-of-ai-in-business-strategies-for-2025-and-beyond

46 J. R. R. Tolkien, *The Hobbit, or There and Back Again* (Boston, MA: Houghton Mifflin Harcourt, 2012), p. 7.

47 Chris Chittock, 'The AI Bubble Will Burst. But It Won't Be Like the Dot-Com Crash', *Pivot Consulting*, 10 December 2025, https://pivot-consulting.com/the-ai-bubble-will-burst/

48 Michael Burry, 'The Cardinal Sign of a Bubble: Supply-Side Gluttony', *Cassandra Unchained*, Substack, 23 November 2025, https://michaeljburry.substack.com/p/the-cardinal-sign-of-a-bubble-supply

both fighting and coexisting. And again, the need for a balance between the two. Is this a chimera? Wishful thinking? Or are there feasible ways to reach this balance? Indeed, in the midst of a great deal of entropy and confusion, we are also starting to see some 'positive deviants'[49] emerging among organisations. These illustrate that an achievable trajectory for AI development exists, aligning innovation with inclusion and sustainability. Many are using maturity models to guide this progress; when anchored in a clear strategy and sound governance, such models can be an invaluable practical tool, as discussed in Chapter 11 in this volume.

AI DISCLAIMER: Giuliano Pozza did not use AI in writing this chapter. However, AI was used by this author for research purposes in collecting supporting evidence. Simon Whittemore did not use AI at all in this chapter.

References

Abhinav, 'The Cost of Intelligence: AI Future is Unsustainable in its Current Form of Growth', *Medium*, 22 October 2025, https://medium.com/@abhinav0231/the-cost-of-intelligence-e55827c7bfeb

'AI & IP: Addressing the Challenges of Data Scraping and the OECD View', *IP Solved*, 19 February 2025, https://ipsolved.com/news/posts/ai-ip-addressing-the-challenges-of-data-scraping-and-the-oecd-view/

Arvind, P., 'Integrity Lost: The Stunning Collapse of Enron's Empire', *AP Thinks*, 15 August 2025, https://apthinks.com/integrity-lost-the-stunning-collapse-of-enrons-empire/

Batool, Amna, Didar Zowghi and Muneera Bano, 'AI Governance: A Systematic Literature Review', preprint, 24 July 2024, https://doi.org/10.48550/arXiv.2401.10896

Bhattacharya, Lipika, 'Why AI's Role in Advancing Sustainability Is Underestimated', *World Economic Forum*, 3 March 2025, https://www.weforum.org/stories/2025/03/can-ai-foster-sustainability/

Blueprint for Business, *The Purpose of Purpose*, https://www.blueprintforbusiness.org/the-purpose-of-purpose/

Bruno, Anna, 'How Artificial Intelligence Helps the *Financial Times* to Moderate the Comments', *annabruno.it* (n.d.), https://www.annabruno.it/en/as-

49 See Prologue for definition and explanation.

artificial-lintellimation-helps-the-financial-times-to-moderate-the-comments/

Burry, Michael, 'The Cardinal Sign of a Bubble: Supply-Side Gluttony', *Cassandra Unchained*, Substack, 23 November 2025, https://michaeljburry.substack.com/p/the-cardinal-sign-of-a-bubble-supply

Aditya Challapally, Chris Pease, Ramesh Raskar and Pradyumna Chari, *The GenAI Divide: State of AI in Business 2025* (Project NANDA, 2025), https://mlq.ai/media/quarterly_decks/v0.1_State_of_AI_in_Business_2025_Report.pdf

Chittock, Chris, 'The AI Bubble Will Burst. But It Won't Be Like the Dot-Com Crash', *Pivot Consulting*, 10 December 2025, https://pivot-consulting.com/the-ai-bubble-will-burst/

de Vries-Gao, Alex, 'The Carbon and Water Footprints of Data Centers and What This Could Mean for Artificial Intelligence', *Patterns*, 7.1 (2025), 101430, https://doi.org/10.1016/j.patter.2025.101430

Direct X, 'OpenAI: The Billion-Dollar Burn—Will It Ever Be Profitable?', *Medium*, 4 November 2025, https://medium.com/%40directX/openai-the-billion-dollar-burn-will-it-ever-be-profitable-536be8c90251

Down, Aisha, '"We could have asked ChatGPT": Students Fight Back Over Course Taught by AI', *The Guardian*, 20 November 2025, https://www.theguardian.com/education/2025/nov/20/university-of-staffordshire-course-taught-in-large-part-by-ai-artificial-intelligence

Guest, Olivia, Marcela Suarez, Barbara Müller et al., 'Against the Uncritical Adoption of "AI" Technologies in Academia', position paper, 13 September 2025, https://doi.org/10.5281/zenodo.17065099

Harari, Yuval Noah, *Nexus: A Brief History of Information Networks from the Stone Age to AI* (London: Fern Press, 2024).

Hautz, Julia, David Seidl and Richard Whittington, 'Open Strategy: Dimensions, Dilemmas, Dynamics', *Long Range Planning*, 50.3 (2017), 298–309 https://doi.org/10.1016/j.lrp.2016.12.001

Hosseinioun, Moh, Frank Neffke, Hyejin Youn and Letian (LT) Zhang, *'Soft Skills Matter Now More Than Ever, According to New Research'*, *Harvard Business Review*, 26 August 2025, https://hbr.org/2025/08/soft-skills-matter-now-more-than-ever-according-to-new-research

Kariuki, Njenga, 'Economy', in N. Maslej, L. Fattorini, R. Perrault et al., *Artificial Intelligence Index Report 2025* (Stanford, CA: Stanford Institute for Human-Centered AI, 2025), https://hai.stanford.edu/ai-index/2025-ai-index-report/economy

Leong, W. Y., 'Artificial Intelligence-Driven Analytics for Monitoring and Mitigating Climate Change Impacts', *Engineering Proceedings*, 108 (2025) 7, https://doi.org/10.3390/engproc2025108007

McKinsey and Company, 'The Economic Potential of Generative AI: The Next Productivity Frontier', 14 June 2023, https://www.mckinsey.com/capabilities/tech-and-ai/our-insights/the-economic-potential-of-generative-ai-the-next-productivity-frontier

Overney, Cassandra, 'Designing for Constructive Civic Communication: A Framework for Human-AI Collaboration in Community Engagement Processes', *arXiv* preprint, 16 May 2025, https://doi.org/10.48550/arXiv.2505.11684

Penrose, E. T., *The Theory of the Growth of the Firm* (New York: John Wiley, 1959).

Ritala, Paavo, Päivi Aaltonen, Mika Ruokonen and Andre Nemeh, 'Developing Industrial AI Capabilities: An Organisational Learning Perspective', *Technovation*, 138 (2024), 103120, https://doi.org/10.1016/j.technovation.2024.103120

Rowland, Sepideh, 'The Identity Dilemma: How AI Blurs the Line Between Reality and Fraud', *The Financial Brand*, 2 January 2026, https://thefinancialbrand.com/news/banking-technology/ai-id-fraud-bank-194966

Samuel, Lawrence R., 'Is Artificial Intelligence a Threat to Personal Identity?', *Psychology Today*, 17 December 2025, https://www.psychologytoday.com/gb/blog/psychology-yesterday/202512/is-artificial-intelligence-a-threat-to-personal-identity

Salatino, Adriana, Arthur Prével, Emilie Caspar and Salvatore Lo Bue, 'Influence of AI Behavior on Human Moral Decisions, Agency, and Responsibility', *Scientific Reports*, 15 (2025), Article 95587, https://doi.org/10.1038/s41598-025-95587-6

Seneca, Lucius Annaeus, *Epistulae Morales ad Lucilium* (Letters to Lucilius), Letter 71.

Stackpole, Beth, 'Agentic AI, Explained', *MIT Management*, 18 February 2026, https://mitsloan.mit.edu/ideas-made-to-matter/agentic-ai-explained

Teece, D., and G. Pisano, 'The Dynamic Capabilities of Firms: An Introduction', *Industrial and Corporate Change*, 3 (1994), 537–556, https://doi.org/10.1093/icc/3.3.537-a

Teece, David J., Gary Pisano and Amy Shuen, 'Dynamic Capabilities and Strategic Management', *Strategic Management Journal*, 18.7 (1997), 509–533.

'The Role of AI in Business Strategies for 2025 and Beyond', *The Strategy Institute*, 13 January 2025, https://www.thestrategyinstitute.org/insights/the-role-of-ai-in-business-strategies-for-2025-and-beyond

Tolkien, J. R. R., *The Hobbit, or There and Back Again* (Boston, MA: Houghton Mifflin Harcourt, 2012).

University of Oxford, 'The Most Prominent UK Business Values Do Not Include Humility or Gratitude—Oxford Study', *University of Oxford*, 4 August 2022, https://www.ox.ac.uk/news/2022-08-04-most-prominent-uk-business-values-do-not-include-humility-or-gratitude-oxford-study

Whittemore, Simon, 'Transversal Competencies for Sustainable Employability — An Overview and a Vade Mecum' (white paper, May 2023).

5. Can AI Help Medicine to Be More Inclusive and Sustainable?

Giuliano Pozza and John D. Halamka

AI and Medicine

The history of AI in medicine is almost as old as AI. I, Giuliano, still remember the smell of the first book on expert systems in medicine I read during my university years and the excitement of discovering computers could not only compute, but reason as well. Or, at least, they could imitate reasoning well enough to do better than humans in many cases. The first milestones, back in the 1970s, were INTERNIST-1, DENDRAL and MYCIN, which simulated expert level reasoning for differential diagnosis, biochemistry and the diagnosis of bacterial infections. In the 1980 and 90s, artificial neural networks and Bayesian networks were used in the clinical field, paving the way to the first 'non-rule-based' applications, such as support to electrocardiogram analysis.

Machine learning and big data, which started to be experimented with during the 70s, spread into the field healthcare after the year 2000; the first fruit of this labour was the dramatic acceleration in speech-to-text applications and diagnostic images analysis. From there on, development continued, spanning machine learning, deep learning, generative AI, more AI-powered diagnostic applications and a growing number of medical devices with embedded AI.[1]

1 For a timeline of AI in medicine, see: https://pmc.ncbi.nlm.nih.gov/articles/PMC11122160/

 https://doi.org/10.11647/OBP.0530.05

Mega-trends in Population Health and Demographics

While AI was taking its first steps, there was a disruptive mega-trend materialising in Western countries: the baby boom, post-World War II and, consequently, the fast ageing of population. In Europe, presently 21.6% of the population is over sixty-five and the percentage will continue to grow in the next years.[2] This trend has several consequences on societies and healthcare systems: the healthcare costs are growing and the demographics are changing fast, both in population and in the healthcare workforce.[3] The latter is at a point of crisis in many countries, and the system sustainability at large could be jeopardised. In the EU there is a projected shortfall of 950,000 healthcare workers by 2030 and so far the solution is, for many countries, to encourage health workforce migrations.[4] This is a typical case of local optimisation leading to global disaster. This is even more true if we consider the global situation: population growth is slowing down all over the world.[5] Even in continents where the number of children per woman is still much greater than two, this number is decreasing fast. It means that in a few decades from now the global population will decrease sharply. Good news? Maybe in the long run but, as usual, when there is a steep transition, the problem lies not in the final state, but in the transition itself.[6] The scenario in front of us is a world with a growing number of old people and a shortage of physicians, nurses and caregivers.

---

2 Eurostat, 'Population Structure and Ageing, Statistics Explained' (European Commission, data extracted February 2025), https://ec.europa.eu/eurostat/statistics-explained/index.php?title=Population_structure_and_ageing

3 Charles H. Jones and Mikael Dolsten, 'Healthcare on the Brink: Navigating the Challenges of an Aging Society in the United States', *npj Aging*, 10.1 (2024) 22,

4 World Health Organization Regional Office for Europe, *Health Workforce Migration in the WHO European Region: Country Case Studies from Albania, Armenia, Georgia, Ireland, Malta, Norway, Republic of Moldova, Romania and Tajikistan* (WHO Regional Office for Europe, 2025), WHO Reference No. WHO/EURO:2025-10839-50611-76542,

5 Note that here the focus is not on the growth of the population, but on the 'speed' of growth (the derivative of the growth), which is decreasing globally. For example in Africa, while the population is still growing, the number of children per woman dropped from over six in the seventies to four in the last years.

6 For a more detailed analysis see: C. Cottarelli, *Senza giri di parole* (Milan: Mondadori, 2025).

Why AI and Population Ageing Are a Good Match

By now maybe some readers are starting to grasp why we are discussing these two trends (AI and demographics) together. The steep increase in patients over sixty-five and those with co-morbidities, together with a worsening shortage of medical personnel, will soon create unsustainable and non-inclusive healthcare systems all over the world. With shrinking resources and growing costs, many nations are already starting to limit access to health services—let alone the many countries where prevention and health assistance is available only for wealthy people. The problem is complex, and the solution will unfortunately not be easy or simple: it will necessarily include many factors, but digital healthcare and AI could be among the most powerful countermeasures. Let us explore how. There are several examples of interesting applications of AI helping the healthcare system, but a good starting point is probably ISM001-055. It is one of the most successful drugs recently discovered and it helped enormously people affected by idiopathic pulmonary fibrosis (IPF), a nasty disease with catastrophic effects. Two aspects of ISM001-055 are remarkable: first, the discovery has been made possible thanks to the pharma.ai platform, built upon diverse AI tools such as PandaOmics, Chemistry42 and inClinico. The second (and at least as important) fact is that it took less than eighteen months for the drug to reach the stage of 'pre-clinical candidate' (PCC), and only 9 months to advance from the PCC stage to the First-in-Human (FIH) milestone! A huge improvement over the standard process, which takes on average ten years or more from the start to FIH stage. This acceleration suggests that the cost of drugs, for which research and development are a major driver, could decrease significantly, increasing the accessibility of new treatments.[7]

But the number of AI applications in healthcare is growing every day, and readers will undoubtedly be able to add much more than we can capture here. Many examples can be found in the experience of the Mayo Clinic Platform,[8] an organisation stemming from the Mayo Clinic

7 'How AI Is Irrevocably Altering the DNA of Drug Development', *DrugPatentWatch*, 20 November 2025,

8 For more details, see Paul Cerrato and John D. Halamka, *Transform: Mayo Clinic Platform and the Digital Future of Health* (Rochester, MN: Mayo Clinic Press/Taylor & Francis Ltd, 2025).

and whose vision is 'to create a healthier world where personalised, predictive, and innovative care is accessible to all'.[9] Diagnostics is one of the fields more impacted by AI. Retinal analysis, endoscopy, digital pathology and ECG analysis can benefit enormously from AI. The number of AI-powered approved medical devices is skyrocketing, as reported by the US Food and Drug Administration (FDA) and illustrated in the Stanford AI Index Report 2025.[10]

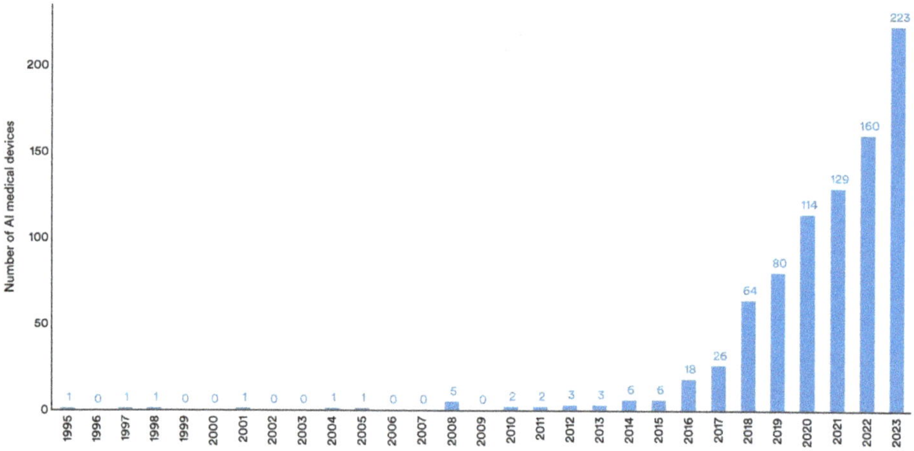

Fig. 5.1 Number of AI medical devices approved by the FDA, 1995–2023. Source: FDA, 2024. Chart: 2025 AI Index Report.

In 2013, there were three AI medical devices approved by the FDA, 114 in 2020, 223 in 2023 and an estimated 235 in 2024. The key point here is not about the numbers, but the increasing rate of AI medical devices approved: +106% from 2020 to 2024. Moreover, most of the EHR (Electronic Health Record) vendors are integrating machine learning or other AI tools in their products to improve Decision Support Systems (DSS). Population health managers can benefit greatly from AI for data analysis and predictions. Again, the mentioned applications can help create more sustainable and inclusive healthcare.

9 Mayo Clinic Platform, 'About', *Mayo Clinic Platform* (2026), https://www.mayoclinicplatform.org/about/

10 N. Maslej, L. Fattorini, R. Perrault et al., *Artificial Intelligence Index Report 2025* (Stanford, CA: Stanford Institute for Human-Centered AI, 2025), https://hai.stanford.edu/ai-index/2025-ai-index-report

The 'Augmented' Physician

We are starting to see an 'AI-augmented' physician emerging. But 'there are more things in heaven and earth, Horatio, than are dreamt of in your philosophy',[11] so there is more in our future than we can dream of now. AI and robotics will inevitably merge in the next few years and that will revolutionise, for example, the long-term care sector. We still cannot predict how robotic AI-powered caregivers will be accepted by patients, but in the future in many retirement homes, the elderly could be the only humans left. Scary? Maybe but, in a broader sense, the extensive use of technology could help democratise care, making it more sustainable and affordable (and therefore inclusive), including for lower income families, communities and countries. Of course, we are advocating for a human-centred healthcare and long-term care ecosystem, with a dominant role of humans in using and governing AI and robotics. However, what we advocate for does not matter so much in the long run, and maybe even in the short. It is better to start thinking about how to govern this complexity now, to avoid dystopic scenarios.

Lightness and Weight

The first point we need to realise about our future is that there is an intrinsic complexity in introducing AI tools in techno-human settings. Even if the tool is as 'simple' as a chatbot, where there is a command line for input and a text output, everything happening in natural language, the outcomes and the side effects could be quite unpredictable. Technology is just one of the actors of a very complex theatrical piece. In this play, the relationships and the interactions among different actors are crucial. Only the collaboration between physicians, healthcare professionals at large, patients, caregivers, pharmaceutical industry, regulatory systems and governance can build a truly effective, sustainable and inclusive healthcare system. But for this collaboration to be effective, a massive cultural shift is needed, not only in terms of training and consideration of dystopic scenarios. But probably, the real game changer will be our capability (or the absence of it) to govern AI in effective ways. And

11 William Shakespeare, *Hamlet*, in *The Oxford Shakespeare: The Complete Works* (Oxford: Oxford University Press, 2008), Act I, Scene 5, lines 166–167.

speaking of governance, the attentive reader should have noticed that the actors mentioned so far are not the only ones involved in the play. Increasingly, the major technology companies are defining our future, not only in healthcare. The investments are huge, the stakes high, and medicine is a strategic battlefield for many of big techs. This is, at the same time, good and bad news. In the past, governments , universities and public research institutions led the way. With AI, we play a different game. The impression is that the industry giants are moving quite freely. Regulatory actors are important as well, such as the AI Act in Europe, but the balance between innovation, ethics and sustainability is a difficult one. Too many regulations and you miss the opportunities behind AI; not enough regulations and you end up in a dystopic future. And we must be conscious that everything we mentioned could be reversed to its 'dark side'. AI for the pharmaceuticals could be used to engineer new and lethal viruses. And we are not speaking of computer viruses. The idea of genetic or ethnic bioweapons is one of the most terrifying dystopic scenarios we can think of. Technology, data and AI can enable deeper knowledge and awareness, but they can be used as well to manipulate our perception of the world in very powerful ways.[12] AI-powered clinical decision support (CDS) tools can greatly enhance both patient and population health, but could embed dangerous biases. And the bad news is that, as some studies are demonstrating, the biases will persist even if AI is removed from clinical practice.[13] The same holds true for diagnostic tools: are we sure that the foundation models we use for endoscopy or digital pathology have the same accuracy for Caucasian and non-Caucasian patients? But probably one of the main issues with AI in medicine nowadays is the risk of deskilling among young medical professionals: studies demonstrate that using AI extensively could impact negatively on medical skills in two ways: deskilling and upskilling inhibition.[14]

12 Mario Escribano, 'Todo empezó en Trinidad y Tobago: la estrategia para "aumentar la apatía" que ahora usa el PP se probó en ese país en 2010', *elDiario.es*, 5 September 2019.

13 Lucía Vicente, Helena Matute, Caterina Fregosi and Federico Cabitza, 'Machine Learning Systems as Mentors in Human Learning: A User Study on Machine Bias Transmission in Medical Training', *International Journal of Human-Computer Studies*, 198 (2025), 103474, https://doi.org/10.1016/j.ijhcs.2025.103474

14 C. Natali, L. Marconi, L. D. Dias Duran, A. et al., 'AI-induced Deskilling in Medicine: A Mixed-Method Review and Research Agenda for Healthcare and

We explored the two faces of the coin of AI in medicine, lightness and weight. There is not a final conclusion, but probably we should simply accept the idea that the future we can foresee now is both risky and exciting. The role of physicians is changing fast, and they are already becoming a sort of augmented version of themselves. There are a number of 'positive deviants'[15] who are using AI to streamline repetitive and predictable tasks, so they can focus on the real challenges: hard-to-detect diagnoses, experimental therapies, intuitive discoveries. A physician working with AI can outperform the physician alone, as a study from Beth Israel Deaconess Medical Center shows.[16] We will need to leverage these tools to reinvent healthcare, as Christensen anticipated in his 'Innovator's Prescription'.[17] Many of the ideas that Christensen proposed then are more achievable now than when he wrote his book, thanks to advances in AI and robotics. The disruption is already here, and it is a big wave: we must decide if we want to be overwhelmed by it or if we can find a reasonable way to surf the wave. But we will need to invest heavily in the reshaping of our organisations (see Chapter 4 in this volume), digital culture, training, governance infrastructures and tools to make the best of what is happening now. In the past, hyperbolic adjectives such as transformation, disruption, revolution were often associated with the digital world. It is now time to avoid hyperboles and to work pragmatically on how to build a constructive relationship with machines that, in healthcare as in other areas, will contribute substantially to shape our future. Machines, in the form of AI, robots or AI-empowered robots, are here to stay. Better to start now developing a healthy relationship with them!

AI DISCLAIMER: the authors did not use AI in writing this chapter. However, AI was used for research purposes in collecting supporting evidence.

Beyond', *Artificial Intelligence Review,* 58 (2025) 356.

15 See the Prologue for context and definitions.

16 Jacqueline Mitchell, 'Better Together: Physicians Using AI Showed Improved Performance in Randomized Controlled Trial', *Beth Israel Deaconess Medical Center,* 5 February 2025.

17 Clayton M. Christensen, Jerome H. Grossman and Jason Hwang, *The Innovator's Prescription: A Disruptive Solution for Health Care* (New York: McGraw-Hill, 2008).

References

Cerrato, Paul, and John D. Halamka, *Transform: Mayo Clinic Platform and the Digital Future of Health* (Rochester, MN: Mayo Clinic Press/Taylor & Francis Ltd, 2025).

Christensen, Clayton M., Jerome H. Grossman and Jason Hwang, *The Innovator's Prescription: A Disruptive Solution for Health Care* (New York: McGraw-Hill, 2008)

Escribano, Mario, 'Todo empezó en Trinidad y Tobago: la estrategia para "aumentar la apatía" que ahora usa el PP se probó en ese país en 2010', *elDiario.es*, 5 September 2019,

Hirani, R., K. Noruzi, H. Khuram et al., 'Artificial Intelligence and Healthcare: A Journey through History, Present Innovations, and Future Possibilities', *Life*, 14.5 (2024), 557. https://doi.org/10.3390/life14050557

Eurostat, 'Population Structure and Ageing, Statistics Explained' (European Commission, data extracted February 2025),

'How AI Is Irrevocably Altering the DNA of Drug Development', *DrugPatentWatch*, 20 November 2025,

Jones, Charles H., and Mikael Dolsten, 'Healthcare on the Brink: Navigating the Challenges of an Aging Society in the United States', *npj Aging*, 10.1 (2024) 22.

Maslej, N., L. Fattorini, R. Perrault et al., *Artificial Intelligence Index Report 2025* (Stanford, CA: Stanford Institute for Human-Centered AI, 2025), https://hai.stanford.edu/ai-index/2025-ai-index-report

Mayo Clinic Platform, 'About', *Mayo Clinic Platform* (2026), https://www.mayoclinicplatform.org/about/

Mitchell, Jacqueline, 'Better Together: Physicians Using AI Showed Improved Performance in Randomized Controlled Trial', *Beth Israel Deaconess Medical Center*, 5 February 2025.

Natali, C., L. Marconi, L. D. Dias Duran, et al., 'AI-induced Deskilling in Medicine: A Mixed-Method Review and Research Agenda for Healthcare and Beyond', *Artificial Intelligence Review*, 58 (2025) 356.

Shakespeare, William, *Hamlet*, in *The Oxford Shakespeare: The Complete Works* (Oxford: Oxford University Press, 2008).

Vicente, Lucía, Helena Matute, Caterina Fregosi and Federico Cabitza, 'Machine Learning Systems as Mentors in Human Learning: A User Study on Machine Bias Transmission in Medical Training', *International Journal of Human-Computer Studies*, 198 (2025), 103474, https://doi.org/10.1016/j.ijhcs.2025.103474

World Health Organization Regional Office for Europe, *Health Workforce Migration in the WHO European Region: Country Case Studies from Albania, Armenia, Georgia, Ireland, Malta, Norway, Republic of Moldova, Romania and Tajikistan* (WHO Regional Office for Europe, 2025), WHO Reference No. WHO/EURO:2025-10839-50611-76542.

6. From Reaction to Strategy: Navigating the AI Paradox in Higher Education

Anand Padmanabhan

Introduction: The Strategic Pivot

In late 2022, the arrival of generative AI triggered waves of existential anxiety across higher education. Higher education did not 'choose' generative AI; rather, it was abruptly forced into a relationship with it. When widely accessible tools surged into classrooms and workflows, the sector's first response was largely defensive: urgent statements about academic integrity, attempts to interpret what the technology meant for assessment, and a scramble to define what should be allowed, discouraged or prohibited. At that moment, the dominant institutional posture was understandably reactive. In the terms laid out in this volume's Prologue, that was the moment the early 'lightness' of experimentation began to give way to the 'weight' of consequences and responsibility.

In 2024, the conversation has matured, although it remains unsettled. We are no longer in the 'panic' phase; we have entered the 'strategy' phase. What many campuses now face is not a single crisis but a strategic decision: whether AI will be treated as an episodic disruption managed through policy memos or as a structural capability that reshapes pedagogy, student support, and institutional operations. This pivot, from what faculty sometimes described as 'panic' to what leaders increasingly describe as 'strategy', is visible in the tone of recent cross-sector and education-specific analyses. Rather than focusing only on novelty or threat, current

 https://doi.org/10.11647/OBP.0530.06

guidance emphasises execution: selecting use cases, building capacity, and translating experimentation into a repeatable practice.

Yet strategy in higher education rarely means 'uniform adoption'. To navigate this effectively, we must move beyond the binary of 'ban versus embrace' and adopt the posture of what this book's Prologue calls the 'sceptical believer'. That posture matters because it refuses a false choice, holding together both the light(ness) and the weight of AI as we decide how to govern it. A fundamental reality is that institutions do not begin with the same baseline. Differences in budgets, staffing, data maturity, procurement capacity and culture produce uneven readiness levels. Several analyses have described an emerging divide: a gap not only in access to tools but also in the ability to implement them responsibly and at scale. In other words, strategic pivoting is not simply a matter of deciding to use AI; it is a matter of determining whether a university can build the governance and support systems required to use it well.

This chapter focuses on this strategic moment. It explores the tension at the heart of the campus debate, efficiency versus education, and offers implementation frameworks that foreground readiness, governance, and ecosystem support. The argument is straightforward: scaling AI without anchoring it in human-centred design and institutional guardrails risks accelerating the 'logistics' of higher education while weakening the learning mission that justifies the institution in the first place.

The Tension: Efficiency vs Education

Acknowledging the Fears: Deskilling, Surveillance and the 'Logistics' Mindset

The most durable controversies surrounding AI in higher education are not merely technical; they are philosophical. They raise questions about the purpose of a university, what constitutes learning, and how trust is established between faculty and students.

One fear is deskilling. If students can outsource drafting, summarising, translating and problem-solving to a generative system, the concern is not simply that the work becomes easier; it is that essential cognitive practices disappear. What happens to the slow struggle through ambiguity that builds writing ability, mathematical reasoning, conceptual fluency or disciplinary judgment? These concerns recur frequently in faculty-oriented research, where instructors describe both curiosity and unease: excitement about tutoring and feedback, paired with a fear that students will bypass the intellectual labour that lies at the heart of learning.

Another fear is that of surveillance. When institutions feel threatened, they often respond by monitoring. In the early days of generative AI, some campuses leaned toward detection and enforcement of academic dishonesty. This impulse can expand into broader surveillance: proctoring, analytics that infer engagement, and tools that claim to measure authenticity. Even when justified as a safeguard for learning, surveillance can erode the relational trust that makes learning possible. It also risks creating a classroom climate oriented toward compliance rather than curiosity.

These dynamics intersect with a third concern: the 'logistics' mindset. Universities are under pressure to respond to resource constraints, enrolment volatility and rising expectations for student services. AI's operational promise of faster support, automated writing, triage of inquiries and administrative efficiencies, can be deeply appealing. But if the institution's primary AI story becomes 'doing more with less', the learning mission can become secondary. A discussion of scaling AI argued that even well-intended institutional moves often remain locked into legacy assumptions: the new tools end up serving the old metrics (grades, exams, throughput) rather than supporting a reimagining of what students should be able to do in a world where AI is ubiquitous.

The tension, then, is not whether AI improves productivity in education; it often does. The deeper concern is whether productivity will become the dominant value. When efficiency becomes the primary focus, students can be viewed as workflows to optimise, and learning becomes a by-product. A strategic approach must take this tension seriously, rather than treating it as a resistance to innovation.

The Critical Importance of Human-centred Design

The clearest way to resolve this tension is to insist on a human-centred design approach. In education, 'human-centred' means more than just user-friendly interfaces. This means protecting student agency, designing for equity and accessibility, and ensuring that pedagogy, not convenience, drives adoption. International guidance has emphasised these concerns: the need for human-centred implementation, careful governance, attention to privacy and regulation gaps, and ethical validation in educational contexts. Within higher education, this translates into a practical design question that should sit at the centre of any institutional AI initiative:

> Does the use of AI replace the learner's thinking, or does it expand the learner's capacity to think?

This single question shifts the conversation. This moves AI away from being a shortcut and toward being a scaffold. It reframes AI as a learning partner in the hands of the student and instructor, rather than merely a productivity layer imposed by the institution. It turns faculty concerns into design requirements: transparency at the point of use, informed consent, clarity about what data are collected, and assessment practices that still measure meaningful learning in an AI-permeated environment.

Human-centred design also requires humility about what AI cannot do well. AI tools can sound confident even when wrong; they can reproduce bias; they can obscure sources and reasoning. When institutions treat AI outputs as neutral or authoritative, they risk creating new forms of misinformation and inequity, which is precisely the opposite of what higher education is meant to cultivate. The strategic challenge is not to prohibit tools outright but to shape their use so that students learn to interrogate, verify and think with them rather than surrender judgment to them.

Strategic Frameworks for Implementation

Moving from 'AI interest' to sustainable practice requires a framework that recognises AI as a socio-technical change. It simultaneously affects culture, pedagogy, governance and infrastructure. A useful way to organise the implementation is through three interlocking domains:

1. readiness (data + people),
2. governance (guardrails), and
3. delivery (deployment into authentic institutional workflow).

This aligns with recent maturity models emphasising that responsible AI adoption depends not only on technology but also on skills and governance, with data maturity as the foundational layer.

Assessing Readiness (Data + People)

Data readiness is often misunderstood. It does not simply mean 'we have data'. It means that institutions can use data ethically, securely and in ways that align with educational values. Many of the most promising AI applications in higher education, advising support, early alerts, accessibility enhancements, and student service automation touch sensitive student information. Therefore, readiness includes questions of data stewardship, retention, access controls and clarity about which data can be used for which purposes.

In practice, data readiness can be assessed through an inventory that asks the following questions:

- What data would this use case require, and who owns them?
- Are the data accurate and appropriately contextualised?
- What are the privacy expectations and legal constraints?
- Will vendors retain or train on institutional data, and what contract protections exist for this?

People readiness is equally decisive and often more difficult. Faculty and staff vary widely in terms of AI familiarity, confidence and trust. Faculty-focused research indicates that even those who support AI's potential often request clearer guidance, discipline-relevant resources, and practical models for integrating AI literacy into the curriculum. This is important because adoption is not a technical event; it is a professional learning journey. Without support, adoption becomes uneven: a few innovators experiment while many others opt out or resist quietly.

A strategic readiness process benefits from a simple prioritisation lens: evaluate proposed use cases on *instructional value* (how much they deepen learning, feedback, inclusion, or accessibility) and *risk exposure* (data sensitivity, high-stakes decisions, potential harm). This lens helps institutions sequence adoption responsibly, starting with high-value, low-risk implementations while building the governance capacity required for more sensitive domains.

Governance: Building the 'Guardrails'

The phrase 'AI governance' can sound bureaucratic, but in higher education, it is better understood as a trust-based infrastructure. Governance is what enables scaling without compromising safety, equity or institutional values. Executive-level guidance on AI governance emphasises the central dilemma: AI's democratisation and scalability create enormous value potential, but they also amplify risk, making governance, not merely policy, essential to mitigate these risks.

For higher education, guardrails typically need to address the following five domains:

1. *Purpose and scope.* Institutions must define which uses are encouraged (e.g., formative feedback, accessibility support, faculty productivity tools) and which require heightened review (e.g., automated decisions about admissions, financial aid or progression). Guardrails should explicitly prohibit uses that undermine trust or cause unacceptable harm.
2. *Data and privacy.* Clear guidance is needed on what information should never be entered into tools, what can be used with approved platforms, and how retention and model-training restrictions are managed.
3. *Academic integrity and assessment alignment.* A sustainable strategy moves beyond 'cheating rules' toward an assessment design that remains valid when AI becomes widely available. Sector efforts to compile and share institutional policy models underscore this shift toward multilevel approaches that integrate institutional direction with local pedagogical practices.
4. *Equity, bias and accessibility.* Institutions must adopt requirements for bias evaluation and accessibility reviews, especially when AI influences student outcomes.
5. *Transparency and accountability.* Students and faculty require clarity on where AI is utilised, how outputs should be interpreted, and who is responsible when AI contributes to errors or harm.

Governance also requires an operational model. Many institutions formed task forces and offered workshops in the early wave of adoption; these were necessary first steps, but they often lacked a long-term structure that could sustain decisions over time. A workable model typically includes a central governance council spanning academic leadership, IT, privacy/legal, accessibility and student representation, paired with school or departmental mechanisms that allow for discipline-specific adaptation. This combination protects consistency without forcing a one-size-fits-all approach.

Supporting the Ecosystem

Even the best governance framework will fail if faculty and staff do not have practical support to implement AI in ways that advance learning. The challenge of scale is, at its core, a challenge of capacity. Support is how institutions cultivate 'positive deviants', individuals who use the same tools not as shortcuts, but as a means to deepen their capability and judgment. Adoption requires professional development, time, incentives and accessible tools.

The guidance emphasises multi-level action planning and professional learning as central to the sector's next phase. Faculty-focused research reinforces that message: instructors want help not only with the mechanics of AI tools but also with redesigning learning outcomes, assignments and integrity norms in ways that fit their disciplines.

A scalable support ecosystem typically includes three components:

Training as a Pathway, not an Event

Effective support is layered as follows:

- baseline AI literacy for everyone (limitations, hallucinations, bias, privacy),
- pedagogical integration support for instructors (assessment redesign, student AI literacy, feedback practices), and
- role-based training for staff (advising, student services, communications and institutional research).

Incentives that Acknowledge the Labour of Redesign

Course redesign requires time. Institutions can signal that this work matters through teaching innovation mini-grants, stipends for redesign cohorts, recognition in promotion or teaching awards, and workload acknowledgment for those developing reusable templates and learning artifacts.

Native Deployment as an Equity and Scale Strategy

One of the strongest recent scaling moves is leveraging generative AI capabilities already embedded in enterprise platforms. The advantage is not merely convenience; it can also improve equity of access by reducing reliance on students purchasing premium accounts. When tools are deployed natively within existing systems, faculty and students encounter them where work already happens, that is, inside productivity suites, learning platforms, or approved institutional environments.

That said, 'native' does not mean 'risk-free'. Embedded tools can accelerate adoption faster than policies can keep up, and they may introduce unclear data pathways. Native deployment is therefore most effective when paired with clear guardrails: what data are prohibited, what disclosures are expected, and how outputs should be validated.

A Human-centred AI Future

The higher education sector's strategic pivot is real, but its direction is not predetermined. Institutions can choose to use AI primarily to accelerate institutional workflows or strengthen learning, inclusion and student agency. The difference is not the technology but the design philosophy and the support ecosystem that surrounds it.

A human-centred AI future requires striking a balance between the scale of AI and the intimacy of teaching. Put differently, we cannot choose between lightness and weight: we need the benefits of scale while carrying the ethical and human responsibility that makes learning real. Teaching is a relational process that relies on trust, a sense of belonging, motivation, feedback and subtle cues that signal to students that they are valued and seen. In contrast, AI scales easily. This mismatch creates the temptation to 'solve' educational challenges through automation. However, the most credible guidance emerging from thought leadership suggests that human-centred adoption depends on building a coordinated institutional ecosystem: data maturity, skills and professional learning, technology choices that support equitable access, and governance structures that keep human values in the loop.

Perhaps the most useful way to summarise this strategic moment is as follows: higher education must ensure that AI does not become the invisible author of student work or the silent governor of student opportunity. It must instead become a tool that students learn to interrogate and use ethically, an instrument for creativity, feedback, accessibility and deeper learning.

The task ahead is not to preserve a pre-AI university environment. It is to build a university that remains worthy of trust in an AI-shaped world: rigorous in its thinking, transparent in its systems, and human in its commitment.

AI DISCLAIMER: the author did not use AI in writing this chapter.

References

EdTech Magazine, 'How Higher Ed Institutions Are Using Built-In Generative AI Tools', 3 June 2025, https://edtechmagazine.com/higher/article/2025/06/how-higher-ed-institutions-are-using-built-generative-ai-tools

EDUCAUSE, *2025 EDUCAUSE Horizon Report: Teaching and Learning Edition*, 12 May 2025, https://library.educause.edu/resources/2025/5/2025-educause-horizon-report-teaching-and-learning-edition

EDUCAUSE, '2025 Horizon Action Plan: Building Skills and Literacy for Teaching with GenAI', 29 September 2025, https://library.educause.edu/resources/2025/9/2025-educause-horizon-action-plan-building-skills-and-literacy-for-teaching-with-genai#:~:text=Monday%2C%20September%2029%2C%202025%20Briefs,future%20we%20want%20to%20see.

Jisc, 'A Strategic Framework for AI in Colleges and Universities', 28 August 2025, https://nationalcentreforai.jiscinvolve.org/wp/2025/08/28/a-strategic-framework-for-ai-in-colleges-and-universities/

Jisc, 'Artificial Intelligence (AI) in Tertiary Education', 26 April 2021, updated 6 September 2023, https://www.jisc.ac.uk/reports/artificial-intelligence-in-tertiary-education

Ithaka S+R, 'Making AI Generative for Higher Education', 1 May 2025.

Brookings Institution, 'Bias in Predictive Analytics for Higher Education Student Success', 17 April 2025, https://www.brookings.edu/articles/using-ai-to-predict-student-success-in-higher-education/

OECD, 'Trends Shaping Education 2025', 23 January 2025, https://www.oecd.org/en/publications/trends-shaping-education-2025_ee6587fd-en/full-report/global-trends-and-the-future-of-education-in-2025_7358e77a.html

Times Higher Education Campus, 'Scaling Generative AI Adoption in Higher Education', 09 December 2025, https://www.timeshighereducation.com/campus/scaling-ai-adoption-higher-education

US Department of Education, Office of Educational Technology, 'Artificial Intelligence and Future of Teaching and Learning: Insights and Recommendations', May 2023, https://www.ed.gov/sites/ed/files/documents/ai-report/ai-report.pdf

UNESCO, 'Reflections on Generative AI and the Future of Education', July 2023, https://doi.org/10.54675/HOXG8740

7. AI and the Future of Work

Bianca de Teffé Erb

The single most important thing to know about AI and the future of work is that it is not about humans versus AI: it is about humans with AI.

For decades, headlines have warned us about 'robots taking our jobs'. This frame misses a crucial nuance: AI does not replace jobs wholesale; it automates specific tasks within those jobs. Understanding this distinction is essential because it reveals that the future of work is not a binary choice between light and dark, human or machine, but rather a spectrum of collaboration between the two.

Consider how work will evolve: rather than the ominous 'AI is replacing humans', we are witnessing a redistribution of work along a spectrum of human–AI interaction, as the following figure illustrates:

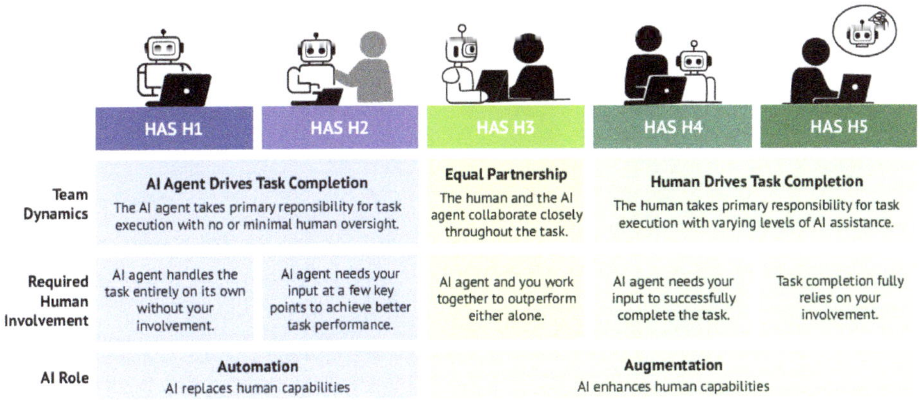

Fig. 7.1 Levels of Human Agency Scale (HAS), from Shao et al., 'Future of Work with AI Agents (2024).[1]

1 Y. Shao, H. Zope, Y. Jiang, J. Pei, D. Nguyen, E. Brynjolfsson and D. Yang, 'Future of

 https://doi.org/10.11647/OBP.0530.07

This spectrum ranges from full human control to full AI automation, with multiple degrees of partnership in between. Only when every task comprising a job becomes automated can we truly say 'AI eliminates that job'. While such cases exist—elevator operators of the past, perhaps drivers in the future—these do represent a small fraction of the labour market. Research across twenty-one OECD countries shows that only 9% of jobs are fully automatable.[2] Vice versa, when humans and AI work closely together (levels H3 and H4 on the scale) they deliver the strongest productivity gains, combining machine efficiency with human judgment, oversight and contextual understanding.[3]

Here, an interesting fact is that workers welcome AI taking over repetitive and low-value tasks.[4] Who genuinely wants to spend hours formatting a document or converting file formats? AI has the power to free up significant worker time and create space for work that is essential to society's functioning—caregiving, household management, family support—which currently is unpaid and falls disproportionately on women.[5]

We are not passive recipients of this evolution. We have both the ability and responsibility to decide which tasks operate at each level of the scale.

Five Lessons from the Past

History shows us that our predecessors have faced similar technological transitions and were able to navigate through them. The introduction of AI represents another chapter in this ongoing story, not an unprecedented

Work with AI Agents: Auditing Automation and Augmentation Potential across the U.S. Workforce', *arXiv* (2024), https://doi.org/10.48550/arXiv.2506.06576

2 M. Arntz, T. Gregory and U. Zierahn, *The Risk of Automation for Jobs in OECD Countries: A Comparative Analysis*, OECD Social, Employment and Migration Working Papers, No. 189 (Paris: OECD Publishing, 2016), p. 7, https://doi.org/10.1787/5jlz9h56dvq7-en

3 Kevin Schaul, 'Can AI Do Your Job? See the Results from Hundreds of Tests', *The Washington Post* (8 January 2026), https://www.washingtonpost.com/technology/interactive/2026/ai-jobs-automation/

4 Examples of repetitive and low-value tasks include: schedule appointments, file management, issue and record adjustments, read and interpret reports, prepared and monitor budgets. Shao, Zope, Jiang et al. 'Future of Work with AI Agents'.

5 Caroline Criado Perez, *Invisible Women: Data Bias in a World Designed for Men* (New York: Abrams Press, 2019).

crisis. By learning from past transitions, we can avoid repeating mistakes and design a future that works for everyone.

As Winston Churchill observed: 'The longer you can look back, the farther you can look forward'.[6]

1. History Repeats Itself

From past innovations[7] to AI, new technologies move through similar phases of adoption and workforce impact, as illustrated below.

Fig. 7.2 Technology adoption and workforce impact phases. Created by the author (2026).

One such examples is driver-assist technologies, such as adaptive cruise control and lane-keeping assistance, which were introduced to improve road safety and reduce driver workload (illustrated as 'Emergence' in the figure). Early systems functioned only under specific conditions, were costly, and poorly understood, which led many drivers to distrust them. As these features became more widespread, reactions quickly polarised (illustrated as 'Hype & Fear in the figure). Some drivers welcomed them as a safety breakthrough, while others worried: 'Can I really trust the car to brake or steer for me?'. With broader adoption, limitations became evident ('Skills Shift'). Misuse and accidents highlighted that this tech does not replace human responsibility, requiring new habits and awareness from drivers. In response, regulators established classifications, such as the Levels of

6 Winston S. Churchill, speech to the Royal College of Physicians, London, 2 March 1944.

7 Examples of technological innovations that have gone through the standard phases include: mobile and wearable contactless payments; facial recognition systems used for security purposes; keyless access technologies (unlocking cars, homes, or offices without physical keys); real-time navigation apps; smart devices.

Driving Automation, stating that driver-assist technologies require mandatory human supervision ('Institutional Adaptation'). Today, driver-assist features are standard in many vehicles and are widely accepted ('Augmentation & Productivity').

2. Fear and Hype Fade

Historically, anxiety peaked in early adoption phases, when workers did not yet know how new technologies would affect their tasks (unawareness) or what alternatives existed (uncertainty).[8] Predictions of mass unemployment were common—and consistently overstated.[9] As practical uses, alternative jobs and the main work impact became clearer, fear subsided. Hype followed a predictable cycle. Early technological waves were accompanied by inflated expectations (bubbles)[10] that later collapsed as limits, costs and trade-offs emerged. What followed was something quieter: normalisation. Technologies became embedded in everyday work. AI is no different—the challenge is not the bubble but guiding the transition once it bursts.

3.Technology Has Made Jobs Less Hazardous and Better Paid

The evidence is striking: in 1870, over 60% of the workforce was engaged in physically demanding and dangerous jobs; by 1970, this dropped to 9%.[11] In agriculture, when tractors replaced horses, it saved a whopping

8 Historical example is represented by the Luddites, nineteenth-century English textile workers who destroyed mechanised looms out of fear that machines would displace skilled labour and undermine wage.

9 K. Hötte, M. Somers and A. Theodorakopoulos, 'Technology and Jobs: A Systematic Literature Review', *Technological Forecasting and Social Change*, 190 (2023), 122750, https://doi.org/10.1016/j.techfore.2023.122750

10 History shows that waves of technological enthusiasm, often described as 'bubbles', have emerged repeatedly, as seen in cases such as the British Railway Mania of the 1840s (Andrew Odlyzko, 'Collective Hallucinations and Inefficient Markets: The British Railway Mania of the 1840s', 15 January 2010, https://dx.doi.org/10.2139/ssrn.1537338) and the dot-com bubble of the 1990s (Robert J. Shiller, *Irrational Exuberance* (Princeton, NJ: Princeton University Press, 2000)), typically followed by phases of correction, consolidation, and more sustainable adoption.

11 C. B. Frey, *The Technology Trap: Capital, Labor, and Power in the Age of Automation* (Princeton, NJ: Princeton University Press, 2019).

3.4 billion man-hours.[12] In Britain, between 1840 and 1900, productivity increased around 90%, and wages rose by 120%.[13]

4. Workers Who Learned New Skills Stayed Employed

During industrialisation and computer adoption, workers who learned to operate machines or use digital tools remained productive and employable.[14] Job titles evolved, and skill adaptation determined who benefited from technological change.

5. Companies that Invested in Training and Redesign Performed Better

Organisations that combined technology adoption with workforce training and process redesign achieved higher productivity and more stable employment than those that focused solely on replacing human labour. In the early 1980s, sociologist Shoshana Zuboff studied a paper mill that introduced computerised process control systems.[15] She compared approaches to technological adoption and the difference was evident: when workers understood the technology rather than simply being supervised by it, productivity gains were higher and work became more skilled rather than redundant.

These five lessons show clearly that technology reshapes work—it does not end it. Skills, jobs, and workplace structures evolve with each technological wave. This evolution is not predetermined; it is shaped by deliberate choices about education, economic policy, workplace design and institutional support. AI is no exception. Understanding how skills, roles, and work structures are evolving today allows us to shape the future.

12 Ibid.

13 R. C. Allen, 'Engels' Pause: Technical Change, Capital Accumulation, and Inequality in the British Industrial Revolution', *Explorations in Economic History*, 46 (2009), 418–435, https://doi.org/10.1016/j.eeh.2009.04.004

14 Historical evidence of workers who acquired new technological skills, remaining productive and employable, is exemplified in the early 1960s by Dorothy Vaughan, pioneering mathematician and supervisor at NASA who championed her team and mastered new computer programming (FORTRAN) to maintain their central role as computation shifted from human 'computers' to machines. This history is documented in Margot Lee Shetterly's *Hidden Figures* movie.

15 Shoshana Zuboff, *In the Age of the Smart Machine: The Future of Work and Power* (New York: Basic Books, 1988).

Skills: What Is Changing?

'Only tech experts will have jobs in the AI era'. This statement is false. AI is multidisciplinary. It requires technical, humanistic and legal skills, creating opportunities across all backgrounds.

Understanding this opens the door to navigating what's changing in the skill landscape:

- Skills becoming **less critical.** Certain capabilities are moving from 'nice to have' to 'AI will handle it': copying information between systems, translating straightforward text, drafting routine emails, retrieval of data from apps or databases, performing repetitive tasks. You do not need to become an expert at what machines do better.
- Skills needed **right now.** Success today means being fluent in both worlds—human and AI. This requires practical abilities: understanding what each AI tool is designed for, its limitations, and how to use it properly ('AI literacy'); learning to communicate clearly so AI understands what you actually want ('prompting'); staying sceptical ('sceptical believer', as quoted in the Prologue of this volume) by always checking outputs for errors, biases or 'hallucinations' before trusting them ('critical thinking'); and being the bridge by helping others discover, test and learn new tools while sharing what works ('adaptability and knowledge sharing').
- Skills that make you **irreplaceable**. AI amplifies distinctly human skills: ethical reasoning and decision-making; creative problem-solving with AI as your accelerator; adaptability to continuous change; moral judgment in complex situations; and empathy for building genuine human connection and understanding.

Knowing what skills matter is only the first step. The second step is to assess your current level of readiness to use this new technology and adapt to new operating models (e.g. working in an AI-human hybrid team), as to define targeted learning pathways. Workers who regularly assess their skill gaps and actively address them are significantly more likely to thrive through these technological transitions.[16]

16 Major research institutions (e.g. World Economic Forum—Future of Jobs Report,

Jobs: Evolution, Creation, Redistribution and Displacement

AI's impact on work unfolds through four parallel processes: job evolution, job creation, job redistribution and displacement.

Job evolution happens as existing roles adapt to incorporate AI capabilities. Marketing professionals learn to use AI for content generation and audience analysis. Doctors use AI to interpret medical images (see Chapter 5 in this volume). Teachers employ AI tutoring tools. The core job remains, but the skills and workflows evolve. This is the most common pathway—most workers will not change careers, but they will change how they work.

Job creation emerges as technology matures and new needs become apparent. The internet did not just transform existing jobs, it created entirely new ones that were unimaginable in 1990: social media managers, UX designers, cybersecurity analysts, content creators. AI follows the same pattern, generating demand for roles that did not exist five years ago and do not yet have standardised titles.

Some examples of new jobs include: AI ethicist, specialists who ensure AI systems align with human values, rights and fairness principles; AI testers, professionals who deliberately test and probe AI systems for weaknesses and biases before deployment; human–AI collaboration designers, experts who design optimal task distribution between humans and AI.

Job redistribution and displacement will be uneven across countries, genders and skill levels. Advanced economies are likely to experience faster labour market shifts—both displacement and productivity gains—while emerging economies may face slower disruption but risk being excluded from early benefits. Women and highly educated workers, often employed in AI-exposed service and cognitive roles, face higher displacement risk but also greater opportunities for job transformation and upward mobility. Younger and college-educated workers adapt more easily to AI, whereas older workers are statistically more vulnerable to displacement due to reskilling and mobility barriers.

OECD—Employment Outlook and Skills Outlook), publish annual reports detailing which skills are in demand in the labour market—valuable resources for tracking evolving needs and planning your development.

Working Structure: Teams and AI Agents

Two fundamental shifts are emerging. First, because AI is inherently multidisciplinary, effective teams will require hybrid expertise, combining technical, humanistic and legal knowledge. You will work alongside colleagues who bring computer science, philosophy, sociology, law and domain-specific expertise. No single person needs all these skills; the strength lies in the team's collective capability to address AI's technical, ethical and regulatory dimensions.

Second, workers themselves will have personal AI agents. Imagine mixed teams where humans collaborate with their AI assistants—each person supported by an agent handling specific tasks like scheduling meetings, drafting initial reports, researching information or even communicating with other people's AI agents or company AI systems on your behalf. Need to resolve a billing issue? Your AI agent negotiates with the company's AI agent while you focus on higher-value work.

In this future of human–AI collaboration, the critical question becomes: where do we want human interaction, and where is AI autonomy acceptable? These are not just technical decisions—they are value judgments that reveal what we consider important as individuals and as a society.

A striking phenomenon is emerging in the hospitality industry: humans-as-luxury.[17] As AI automates routine interactions, authentic human connection is becoming something you pay extra for. Low-cost hotels in Japan and China deploy AI-powered systems where robots check you in, chatbots handle requests, automation manages everything. Luxury hotels emphasise human concierges as premium features. This raises profound questions: is this the future we want? Should human attention and care become privileges reserved for those who can afford them?

The Path Forward

As AI reshapes work, we need to stay alert to several emerging risks:

- *Income inequality*: Companies reporting profits from AI are keeping wages flat or even reducing workforce, concentrating

17 Simone Puorto, 'Humans-as-Luxury: The Future of Hospitality in an AI-Driven Age', Hospitality Net, 2 April 2025, https://www.hospitalitynet.org/opinion/4126522/humans-as-luxury-the-future-of-hospitality-in-an-ai-driven-age

benefits among executives and shareholders.[18]

- *Worker monitoring and exploitation*: Some companies now evaluate employees based on how much or how well they use AI tools. Others underpay workers performing data labelling tasks.
- *Job (un)clarity*: Your role might constantly evolve as new tasks and required skills get added without clear boundaries. It can feel like the job keeps expanding with no clear definition of what you are responsible for, while maintaining the same wage.[19]
- *Over-reliance on AI*: humans are far more likely to trust what a machine tells us than to challenge it ('automation bias'), leading to inaccurate AI hindering our work and our critical thinking skills. Imagine a doctor who delegates your diagnoses entirely to AI without exercising their own medical judgment—would you feel safe?

These risks are not inevitable. The future of work will be shaped by decisions made at every level:

Policymakers and society must ensure profit-sharing mechanisms, digital capital taxation, and reduced working hours without reduced pay.[20] AI talent marketplaces, platforms to map workers' capabilities to emerging roles, and AI governance frameworks to ensure worker participation and alignment with social values.

Educators and parents should integrate AI literacy into education from an early age—not just technical skills, but critical thinking, ethical reasoning and adaptability. Young people need to understand both AI's capabilities and its limitations.

Companies must rethink roles and workflows to empower workers rather than surveil them. The goal should be insightful, inventive and informed use of AI—technology that amplifies human judgment rather than replaces it.

---

18 Daron Acemoglu and Pascual Restrepo, 'Tasks, Automation, and the Rise in U.S. Wage Inequality', *Econometrica*, 90.5 (2022), 1973–2016, https://doi.org/10.3982/ECTA19815

19 Zuboff, *In the Age of the Smart Machine*.

20 Ekkehardt Ernst, Rossana Merola and Daniel Samaan, 'Economics of Artificial Intelligence: Implications for the Future of Work', *IZA Journal of Labor Policy*, 9.1 (2019) 35, https://doi.org/10.2478/izajolp-2019-0004

You have agency too. Stay informed about how AI affects your field. Develop functional AI literacy. Share what you learn with colleagues and loved ones. Most importantly, participate in workplace decisions about how AI gets deployed—these choices shape your daily reality.

AI DISCLAIMER: the author used AI for brainstorming concepts that she personally wrote about in the chapter.

References

Acemoglu, Daron, and Pascual Restrepo, 'Tasks, Automation, and the Rise in U.S. Wage Inequality', *Econometrica,* 90.5 (2022), 1973–2016, https://doi.org/10.3982/ECTA19815

Allen, R. C., 'Engels' Pause: Technical Change, Capital Accumulation, and Inequality in the British Industrial Revolution', *Explorations in Economic History*, 46 (2009), 418–435, https://doi.org/10.1016/j.eeh.2009.04.004

Arntz, M., T. Gregory and U. Zierahn, *The Risk of Automation for Jobs in OECD Countries: A Comparative Analysis*, OECD Social, Employment and Migration Working Papers, No. 189 (Paris: OECD Publishing, 2016), https://doi.org/10.1787/5jlz9h56dvq7-en

Ernst, Ekkehardt, Rossana Merola and Daniel Samaan, 'Economics of Artificial Intelligence: Implications for the Future of Work', *IZA Journal of Labor Policy,* 9.1 (2019), 35, https://doi.org/10.2478/izajolp-2019-0004

Frey, Carl Benedikt, *The Technology Trap: Capital, Labor, and Power in the Age of Automation* (Princeton, NJ: Princeton University Press, 2019).

Hötte, K., M. Somers and A. Theodorakopoulos, 'Technology and Jobs: A Systematic Literature Review', *Technological Forecasting and Social Change,* 190 (2023), 122750, https://doi.org/10.1016/j.techfore.2023.122750

Odlyzko, Andrew, 'Collective Hallucinations and Inefficient Markets: The British Railway Mania of the 1840s', 15 January 2010, https://dx.doi.org/10.2139/ssrn.1537338

Perez, C. C., *Invisible Women: Data Bias in a World Designed for Men* (New York: Abrams Press, 2019).

Puorto, Simone, 'Humans-as-Luxury: The Future of Hospitality in an AI-Driven Age', *Hospitality Net*, 2 April 2025, https://www.hospitalitynet.org/opinion/4126522/humans-as-luxury-the-future-of-hospitality-in-an-ai-driven-age

Schaul, Kevin, 'Can AI Do Your Job? See the Results from Hundreds of Tests', *The Washington Post*, 8 January 2026, https://www.washingtonpost.com/technology/interactive/2026/ai-jobs-automation/

Shao, Y., H. Zope, Y. Jiang, J. Pei, D. Nguyen, E. Brynjolfsson and D. Yang, 'Future of Work with AI Agents: Auditing Automation and Augmentation Potential across the U.S. Workforce', *arXiv* (2024), https://doi.org/10.48550/arXiv.2506.06576

Shiller, Robert J., *Irrational Exuberance* (Princeton, NJ: Princeton University Press, 2000).

Zuboff, Shoshana, *In the Age of the Smart Machine: The Future of Work and Power* (New York: Basic Books, 1988).

8. Equality and Ethics for AI

Bianca de Teffé Erb

Artificial intelligence has entered our lives with extraordinary lightness. It works quietly in the background, suggesting what to watch, completing our sentences and choosing the fastest route home. Yet behind this lightness lies a tremendous weight: AI influences who gets a job interview, how students learn, what news we see, and even how governments make decisions.

The Promise and the Peril of AI

AI has a dual nature: it can reduce inequality or amplify it; it can open doors or close them.

The Promises (the Light Side)

AI creates opportunities that were unimaginable only a few years ago:

Improve public transportation: AI can make urban mobility faster, safer and more efficient. The 'City Brain project' in China uses AI and big data from video feeds, GPS tracking and IoT sensors to optimise traffic signals and emergency vehicle routing in real time—reducing travel time by 15% and improving emergency response times by up to 50%.[1]

Accessibility: from voice assistants that read text aloud for people with

1 H. Guo and W. Y. Leong, 'Comparative Review of AI Applications in Urban Transport: Insights from China's City Brain and Singapore's LTA Smart Mobility', *Journal of Innovation and Technology*, 1.7 (2025).

 https://doi.org/10.11647/OBP.0530.08

hearing loss,[2] to apps that describe photos to people with low vision,[3] or speech-to-text tools that support people with dyslexia or who struggle with writing. These are examples of how AI is leveling the playing field.

Water (re)use: water scarcity affects over two billion people globally. AI systems are being used to detect leaks in water distribution networks, optimise irrigation in agriculture, and predict drought conditions with greater accuracy[4]—enabling cities and governments to manage water resources more sustainably and equitably.

Enhance safety: AI can detect frauds in real-time,[5] identify unsafe working conditions through sensors that help prevent accidents and protect lives,[6] detect food contamination,[7] and provide warnings to drivers and cyclists to avoid collisions.[8]

Empower the workplace: AI helps workers acquire new skills[9] (e.g. prompting, validating AI outputs) and enable businesses to automate processes, innovate and grow. A concrete example of this dynamic can be seen in a home-furnishing company that, in 2021, automated its contact centre by replacing routine tasks with

2 Y. Brotosaputro, V. Wang and K. Lim, 'AI-Powered Assistive Technologies for Improved Accessibility', *International Transactions on Artificial Intelligence*, 3.1 (2024), https://doi.org/10.33050/italic.v3i1.645

3 C. Kooli, A. Almulhim and R. Alzahrani, 'AI-driven Assistive Technologies in Inclusive Education', *Sustainable Futures*, 10 (2025), 101042, https://doi.org/10.1016/j.sftr.2025.101042

4 H. Kamyab, T. Khademi, S. Chelliapan et al., 'The Latest Innovative Avenues for the Utilisation of Artificial Intelligence and Big Data Analytics in Water Resource Management', *Results in Engineering*, 20 (2023), 101566.

5 Zaki Rojan, 'Financial Fraud Detection Based on Machine and Deep Learning: A Review', *Indonesian Journal of Computer Science*, 13.3 (2025), https://doi.org/10.33022/ijcs.v13i3.4059

6 S. J. Badhan and R. Samsami, 'Artificial Intelligence (AI) in Construction Safety: A Systematic Literature Review', *Buildings*, 15.22 (2025), 4084, https://doi.org/10.3390/buildings15224084

7 S. Kuppusamy, M. Meivelu, L. Praburaman, M. M. Alam, A. G. Al-Sehemi, and A. K., 'Integrating AI in Food Contaminant Analysis: Enhancing Quality and Environmental Protection', *Journal of Hazardous Materials Advances*, 16 (2024), 100509, https://doi.org/10.1016/j.hazadv.2024.100509

8 Bhavya Vashisht, 'AI for Safety: Enhancing Driver Performance and Reducing Accidents with Intelligent Systems', *Journal of Artificial Intelligence, Machine Learning & Data Science*, 2.3 (2024), 1822–1827, https://doi.org/10.51219/JAIMLD/bhavya-vashisht/404

9 World Economic Forum, *The Future of Jobs Report 2025* (Geneva: WEF, 2025), https://www.weforum.org/publications/the-future-of-jobs-report-2025/

AI. Rather than reducing its workforce, the company retrained around 8,500 employees between 2021 and 2023 to become interior design consultants. By 2022, this new service line generated €1.3 billion in revenue.[10] This case shows how AI can create opportunities and value for businesses.

The Perils (the Heavy Side)

Erosion of privacy: AI systems collect and analyse vast amounts of personal data; people may lose control over how their information is used. In 2025, an AI chatbot was used to generate photo-realistic child sexual abuse material by using publicly available photos without their knowledge or consent.[11]

Lack of transparency: opaque algorithms[12] can make decisions about our lives without explaining how or why they reached them. In 2025, researchers recorded a 31% drop in transparency scores across major AI companies.[13] The main opaque domains include: training data, training compute, how models are used and their impact on society.

Misinformation and manipulation of behaviour: in January 2024, fraudsters using deepfake technology impersonated a company's CFO on a video call, tricking an employee into transferring $25 million.[14] AI can generate images, audio or videos of public figures or friends and family that realistically imitate their appearance and voice, even though they are completely fake ('deepfakes'). These can be used to spread misleading content that can confuse us, and influence our opinions or decisions.

10 Reid, Helen, 'IKEA Bets on Remote Interior Design as AI Changes Sales Strategy', *Reuters*, 13 June 2023, https://www.reuters.com/technology/ikea-bets-remote-interior-design-ai-changes-sales-strategy-2023-06-13/

11 Chris Vallance, 'Elon Musk's Grok AI appears to Have Made Child Sexual Imagery, Says Charity' *BBC News*, 8 January 2026, https://www.bbc.co.uk/news/articles/cvg1mzlryxeo

12 'Opaque algorithms' can be understood in two ways: models whose inner logic and work are unknown due to intentional hidden for proprietary reasons, and technical complexity that make it incomprehensible to humans. L. Floridi and M. Taddeo, M. (Eds.), *A Companion to Digital Ethics* (Hoboken, NJ: John Wiley & Sons, 2025).

13 R. Bommasani et al., *2025 Foundation Model Transparency Index*, Stanford HAI, 2025, https://crfm.stanford.edu/fmti/December-2025/paper.pdf

14 Nadia Naffi, 'Deepfakes and the Crisis of Knowing', *UNESCO*, 27 October, https://www.unesco.org/en/articles/deepfakes-and-crisis-knowing

Hallucination: AI may produce information that seems plausible and makes superficial sense, but is actually incorrect or made up! When these errors go unnoticed, they can lead to wrong decisions, misplaced trust, and produce real harm.

Bias amplification: researchers estimate a global gender credit gap of $17 billion,[15] due to credit-scoring AI systems that are likely to exclude women from loans and financial services. This inequality stems from two main sources: firstly, conscious or unconscious prejudices introduced by designers and developers (women represent only 12% of AI researchers);[16] and secondly, the use of incomplete, or unrepresentative data to train AI, also known as a 'data gap'. A known example of this dynamic is a AI voice recognition system that was found to understand male voices up to 69% more accurately than female voices.[17] This performance gap was due to training datasets containing significantly more male speech samples. This is an example of what researcher Caroline Criado Perez calls the 'gender data gap'.[18] As a result, when women tried to use voice-activated features for hands-free navigation or dictation, the AI misunderstood their commands. Rather than addressing the root cause and fixing the biased product, the female users were advised to 'speak more clearly and at a lower pitch' to improve recognition accuracy, obliging them to change how they naturally speak. This case illustrates how biased data and design choices can translate into unequal outcomes, reinforcing existing disparities.

How AI Really Works

Before describing the steps we can take to reap the promises and avoid the perils of AI, we must understand how these systems work.

Here are three fundamental notions to know.

---

15 Laura Bates, 'How Tech Turned Against Women', *Financial Times Europe*, 21 February 2026, https://www.ft.com/content/60e2a900-8999-46cc-8107-4f468f442aae

16 Ibid.

17 Rachael Tatman, 'Google's Speech Recognition Has a Gender Bias', *Making Noise and Hearing Things*, 12 July 2016, https://makingnoiseandhearingthings.com/2016/07/12/googles-speech-recognition-has-a-gender-bias/

18 Caroline Criado Perez, *Invisible Women: Exposing Data Bias in a World Designed for Men* (London: Chatto & Windus, 2019).

1. AI Does Not Understand the Meaning of Words, It Simply Calculates

Not all AI systems are built the same way, and how they are built determines the level of ethical risk they carry. There are two main types of AI systems:

(1) *AI based on deterministic algorithms* (*rule-based*).[19]

These operate on precise and predefined rules: given the same input, they will always produce the same output. Think of it like a vending machine: press B3, you always get the same snack. Press it a thousand times, the result never changes. The machine does not think about your choice, it simply executes a fixed instruction. In AI, this works the same way: 'every time condition X occurs, execute procedure Y'.

From an ethical standpoint, these systems present relatively low risk for three reasons: they are transparent (the rule is known and documented), auditable (you can always trace why a specific output was produced), and predictable (the same input will always produce the same output). If something goes wrong, you can identify the rule that caused it and fix it. This is what governance frameworks refer to as explainability, and deterministic systems have it by design.

(B) *AI systems based on non-deterministic algorithms* (*statistical probability*).[20]

---

19 Rule-based AI systems, also known as expert systems, operate on predefined IF–THEN logic rules. They are commonly used in applications such as fraud detection, banking compliance, and medical diagnosis. This category includes approaches such as decision trees (e.g. ID3, C4.5), finite state machines (FSM), CLIPS (C Language Integrated Production System) developed by NASA, and Prolog-based logic systems. See Russell, S. J., and P. Norvig, *Artificial Intelligence: A Modern Approach*, 3rd ed. (Upper Saddle River, NJ: Pearson, 2010).

20 Non-deterministic AI systems include: large language models (LLMs) used to generate text, code, and analysis (e.g. GPT-4, Gemini, Claude, Llama); generative adversarial networks (GANs) used to generate synthetic images, video and audio, including deepfakes (e.g. StyleGAN, DeepFaceLab); diffusion models, used to generate high-quality images and videos (e.g. Stable Diffusion, DALL-E, Sora); convolutional neural networks (CNNs) used to generate image and pattern recognition (e.g. ResNet, VGG, EfficientNet); recurrent neural networks (RNNs) and LSTMs used to generate language and sequence processing (e.g. early versions of Google Translate, speech recognition systems); and reinforcement learning systems that learn through trial and error interaction with an environment (e.g. AlphaGo, AlphaFold). All modern LLMs are based on Transformer architecture, introduced by Vaswani, A., N. Shazeer, N. Parmar, J. Uszkoreit, L. Jones, A.N.

These are the ones we interact with most (e.g. chatbots, image generators, video synthesis tools, recommendation engines for music, video and on social media platforms). Rather than following a fixed rule, they are trained to analyse a vast amount of data, identify patterns and calculate the most statistically probable answer.

Try asking a chatbot the same questions several times, and you will notice that it will produce a (slightly) different answer each time.

When a chatbot generates text, it does so by selecting the most likely next unit of language (known as a 'token'),[21] which can be a letter, a syllable or a word. Imagine asking a chatbot to complete the sentence 'Once upon a...'. The chatbot scans through a vast amount of existing texts and calculates which word is statistically most likely to follow:

- 'Once upon a → time' (~98% statistically dominant likelihood)
- 'Once upon a → dream' (~15% rare likelihood)
- 'Once upon a → table' (~2% very rare likelihood)

The chatbot selects 'time' because it has the highest likelihood percentage, not because it actually comprehends and understands the request or context. In five words: AI applies math to words.

From an ethical standpoint, these systems present significantly higher risks. They are opaque (the logic behind any output is not a traceable rule, but the result of billions of statistical calculations), difficult to audit (developers often cannot fully explain a specific output)[22] and unpredictable (the same input can produce different results). This is the structural origin of the risks explored throughout this chapter, including hallucination, data gaps and manipulation.

Gomez, L. Kaiser, and I. Polosukhin, 'Attention Is All You Need', *Advances in Neural Information Processing Systems*, 30 (2017).

21 The term token refers to the basic unit of text that a large language model processes. A token can correspond to a single character, a syllable, or a full word depending on the model's architecture. OpenAI's GPT-4, for instance, processes text in tokens of approximately four characters on average.

22 This challenge has given rise to an entire field of research known as Explainable AI (XAI) dedicated to developing methods that make the outputs of non-deterministic AI systems more interpretable and auditable. Key initiatives include DARPA's XAI Program (launched 2016) and the mandatory explainability requirements for high-risk AI systems introduced under the EU AI Act. Despite significant progress, full interpretability of large language models remains an open research problem. M. Bello, R. Bello, M. M. García et al. 'A Three-level Framework for LLM-enhanced Explainable AI: From Technical Explanations to Natural Language', *Information Systems Frontiers* (2025).

2. AI Is Only as Good as the Data It Trains On[23]

AI can predict liver disease accurately for men—but only for half of women,[24] resulting in women being less likely to be diagnosed and more likely to receive inadequate treatment.

Why is the AI only working halfway? Because of a data gap: the dataset on which the AI was trained did not contain sufficient data on women. When data is incomplete, inaccurate or unrepresentative, the AI inherits this gap, producing distorted and partial results.

This challenge becomes even more acute when we consider the source of the data used for training today's major AI chatbots: the internet. In 2024, researchers found that the largest publicly available and most widely used source for training AI systems[25] contains a significant amount of low-quality, unverified and non-authoritative data.[26] The internet is, by design, a space of free expression, where anyone can publish anything. When you ask AI a question, you are not consulting experts, you are receiving a statistical average across thousands of web pages, authoritative and non-authoritative alike. The AI does not distinguish between a peer-reviewed medical journal and a personal blog.

Asking an AI trained on unfiltered internet data for precise technical advice is like asking a crowd of strangers for a medical diagnosis, some of them may be doctors, but you have no way of knowing which ones, if any at all.

Closing the data gap will change the picture entirely. AI trained on complete, accurate and representative data could detect liver disease equally well in men and women, deliver reliable medical advice regardless of who is asking, and become a useful technology serving all. The data gap is not a permanent condition: it is a solvable problem.

23 In this notion of AI and data, when we refer to AI and its algorithms we are focusing on the non-deterministic typology, therefore those that are not rule-based but based on statistical calculations.

24 Mark Greaves, 'Gender Bias Revealed in AI Tools Screening for Liver Disease', *UCL News*, 11 July 2022, https://www.ucl.ac.uk/news/2022/jul/gender-bias-revealed-ai-tools-screening-liver-disease

25 Especially LLMs used for generating text.

26 Stefan Baack, 'A Critical Analysis of the Largest Source for Generative AI Training Data: Common Crawl', in *Proceedings of the 2024 ACM Conference on Fairness, Accountability, and Transparency (FAccT '24)* (New York: ACM, 2024), pp. 2199–2208.

3. By the People for the People (AI's True Mission)

AI is designed on experiences, assumptions, and blind spots of its developers, which may at times overlook the intended purpose and users of the AI product. The starting point in developing AI must be: who will use it?

Once the intended users are clearly identified, they also must actively participate in the design, development and testing phases. After all, who is better than them to design and test the product? This approach is known as 'user-centred design',[27] 'participatory design'[28] or 'co-design'.[29]

For example, a recent review found that most mobile apps for adults aged over sixty don't consider the needs of ageing users, thus resulting in hard-to-read small text, and complex menus and interfaces.[30] Change is possible. For example, the University of Helsinki is working on more inclusive mobility apps by using data from people of all ages, not just the young and the tech-savvy.[31]

All technology, AI included, must be developed by placing the user(s) and our human needs at the forefront. It is not us who must adapt, it is AI that has to. This is why, understanding how AI works matters deeply for equality and ethics: AI is a mirror of ourselves[32] and of our society—it reflects the choices, culture, biases and values of the people who commission and develop it. Recognising this gives us the power to design AI that does not simply repeat the past but help us

---

27 W. V. Siricharoen, 'Elevating User-centered Design with AI: A Comprehensive Exploration using the AI-UCD Algorithm Framework', *EAI Endorsed Transactions on Context-Aware Systems and Applications*, 10 (2024).

28 S. Hossain and S. I. Ahmed, 'Towards a New Participatory Approach for Designing Artificial Intelligence and Data-driven Technologies', *arXiv* (2021).

29 Kadenhe, N., Al Musleh, M., & Lompot, A. (2025). Human–AI co-design and co-creation: A review of emerging approaches, challenges, and future directions. *Proceedings of the AAAI Symposium Series*, 6(1), 265–270

30 Amouzadeh, E., I. Dianat, J. Faradmal et al., 'Optimizing Mobile App Design for Older Adults: Systematic Review of Age-friendly Design', *Aging Clinical and Experimental Research*, 37 (2025), 248 https://doi.org/10.1007/s40520-025-03157-7

31 'Enhanced Urban Planning for Age-friendly Cities through Disruptive Technologies', *Digital Geography Lab* (University of Helsinki), https://www.helsinki.fi/en/researchgroups/digital-geography-lab/projects/enhanced-urban-planning-for-age-friendly-cities-through-disruptive-technologies

32 'AI is a mirror of ourselves, not as we ought to be or could be, but as we already are and have long been', Shannon Vallor, *The AI Mirror: How to Reclaim Our Humanity in an Age of Machine Thinking* (Oxford: Oxford University Press, 2024), p. 10.

create a brighter future.

Wow, now that was heavy...! Let's take a break for a quick fun fact: human–AI collaboration outperforms both humans and AI working alone.[33] As a matter of fact, there is a growing wave of movies highlighting positive human–AI collaboration: Jarvis in *Ironman*, Joi in *Blade Runner 2049*, TARS in *Interstellar.* So how do we ensure that AI is fair, inclusive, transparent, equal, robust, safe? These are not servile machines or cold calculators, they are depicted as entities that enhance human capability while remaining distinctly non-human. The cultural significance of this trend runs deeper than entertainment: when audiences repeatedly see AI framed as a collaborator rather than a conqueror, it shapes public intuition about what AI *should* be and what we should demand of it.

Our Role and What Actions Can We Take to Ensure Ethical AI

What makes the difference is the choices we make about how to design, govern and use it. AI does not know what is right and what is wrong, it has no moral compass. We do.

AI systems can process huge amounts of information and make decisions faster than any human. But these decisions can have real consequences. We have a moral and civic duty to collectively agree and decide what choices and decisions are OK for machines to make autonomously, and which ones are to be lifted to our human, moral and ethical judgment.

This responsibility also shows up in design choices, such as ethical guardrails. These are rules and safeguards defined by developers and embedded directly into AI systems to ensure ethics by design and by default.[34] They help guide AI behaviour and reduce harm without requiring constant intervention from users (e.g. adopting a polite language by default).

33 M. Vaccaro, A. Almaatouq and T. Malone, 'When Combinations of Humans and AI are Useful: A Systematic Review and Meta-analysis', *Nature Human Behaviour*, 8 (2024), 2293–2303, https://doi.org/10.1038/s41562-024-02024-1

34 K. Šekrst, J. McHugh and J. Rodriguez Cefalu, 'AI Ethics by Design: Implementing Customizable Guardrails for Responsible AI Development' (2024), https://arxiv.org/abs/2411.14442

It doesn't matter where you were born, what you studied, how old you are: everyone has a role to play in shaping how AI impacts society. Ethical AI isn't just about fixing technical glitches; it is about building trust. So, what can you do to make an impact that matters? What role do you want to play? Each of us brings a different perspective, skill set and sphere of influence.

Choose the persona that resonates with you most and contribute to a trustworthy AI:

The Challenger	The Pathfinder	The Builder	The Guardian
Someone who questions, verifies, and challenges information.	**Someone who experiments, explores new technologies.**	**Someone who creates fair, transparent and secure AI.**	**Someone who uses AI to protect, guide, and supports others on how to use it!**
Challenge the output: Never accepts AI answers at face value.	*Test new AI tools:* Tries out free / paid AI products	*Design responsibly:* Creates transparent, fair, safe AI.	*Use AI to enhance—not replace—human well-being.*
Verify the source: Double-check data using independent, trusted references.	*Explore creatively:* Experiments with prompts, different ways to use tools.	*Ensures safety & privacy:* Protect user data and mitigate risks from day one.	*Identifies risks:* Recognize when AI causes harm (bias, emotional fragility).
Spot inconsistencies: Notice unclear answers and asks clarifying questions.	*Provide feedback:* Shares what worked well and what didn't. Shares user tips!	*Enable human oversight:* Build mechanisms so users remain in control.	*Promote healthy digital habits:* Encourages balance and promotes use.

Fig. 8.1 The four AI personas framework. Created by the author (2026).

Here are some examples representing these personas, drawn from fiction and non-fiction, and within and outside of the AI context:

Challengers	Pathfinders	Builders	Guardians
Hermione Granger (Harry Potter)	**Tony Stark** (Iron Man)	**Q** (James Bond)	**Baymax** (Big Hero 6)
Maria Ressa (Journalist)	**Sam Altman** (OpenAI Founder)	**Fei-Fei Li** (AI Scientist)	**Shoshana Zuboff** (Sociologist)

Fig. 8.2 The four AI personas framework. Created by the author (2026).

We have the opportunity and duty to embody at least one, or even several or all these roles. The following scenarios reveal how our engagement with AI can shape smarter, safer and more human-centred outcomes.

A Student Using AI for Homework

- **Challenger:** checks whether the AI explanation is correct by comparing it with the textbook.
- **Pathfinder:** tries new study features (flashcards, summaries, quizzes) and shares with classmates what works best.
- **Builder:** tests the school's AI tool and flags inaccurate outputs and provides feedback that helps reduce hallucinations over time.
- **Guardian:** reminds classmates not to rely entirely on AI as it can provide wrong answers, negatively impact their grades, and encourage them to use AI as a supporting tool.

An Employee Using AI to Prepare a Presentation

- **Challenger:** asks the AI to list the references for the statistics it suggested and checks each one against reliable external sources before including the numbers on the slide.
- **Pathfinder:** experiments with an online AI to generate visuals, drafts and alternative storylines.
- **Builder:** uses a specific AI-based cyber security tool so that sensitive company data stays protected.
- **Guardian:** proof-read the language to be inclusive and accessible for all audiences.

A Small Business Adopting AI for Customer Service

- **Challenger:** reviews AI responses to ensure they are correct and reflect company values.
- **Pioneer:** tries new automation tools, explores several ways users can use them by collaborating with different customers, and gathers feedback to improve the AI.
- **Builder:** builds or customises the chatbot, including target users in the testing.
- **Guardian:** monitors how customers feel about interacting with AI chatbots and provides human support when requested.

Building Equal, Fair and Ethical AI: 5 Principles for Everyone

1. Use diverse and representative data: AI should learn from examples that reflect the real world, not only one group, one gender, one region or one lifestyle.
2. Keep a human in-the-loop: important decisions should not be left fully to algorithms. We must be able to question, correct and choice what decisions are never to be made by an AI.
3. Demand transparency and instructions: we deserve to know how to use AI, when it is being used and how it influences an outcome that affects us directly in a clear manner. It is your right to receive this information from the providers and developers of AI.
4. Test for bias regularly: just like we test cars, medicines or elevators, AI should be tested repeatedly to ensure it works fairly for all groups and leaves no one behind.
5. Take responsibility: blaming 'the algorithm' is not enough. Someone, a team, an institution must be designated, communicated and made to be accountable.

A Closing Reflection: Keeping People at the Centre

AI promises a world of speed, ease, efficiency, and an almost magical lightness. But with this lightness comes responsibility. We are the ones who decide whether AI reflects our past or helps us create a better future. The path to fair and ethical AI isn't easy, but with a Challenger, Pathfinder, Builder and Guardian by our side, it is within our reach. If we design AI with equality and ethics at the centre, we can reduce the heavy weight of structural inequalities and open opportunities for millions. If we ignore these issues, the 'lightness' of AI becomes unbearable—a technology that floats above us while quietly deepening the very divides it could have solved.

In the end, the real power of AI lies not in the code, but in the choices we make.

AI DISCLAIMER: the author used AI for brainstorming concepts that she personally wrote about in the chapter.

References

Amouzadeh, E., I. Dianat, J. Faradmal et al., 'Optimizing Mobile App Design for Older Adults: Systematic Review of Age-friendly Design', *Aging Clinical and Experimental Research*, 37 (2025), 248 https://doi.org/10.1007/s40520-025-03157-7

Baack, S., 'A Critical Analysis of the Largest Source for Generative AI Training Data: Common Crawl', in *Proceedings of the 2024 ACM Conference on Fairness, Accountability, and Transparency* (*FAccT '24*) (New York: ACM, 2024), pp. 2199–2208.

Badhan, S. J., and R. Samsami, 'Artificial Intelligence (AI) in Construction Safety: A Systematic Literature Review', *Buildings*, 15.22 (2025), 4084, https://doi.org/10.3390/buildings15224084

Bates, L., 'How Tech Turned Against Women, *Financial Times Europe*, 21 February 2026, https://www.ft.com/content/60e2a900-8999-46cc-8107-4f468f442aae

Bello, M., R. Bello, M. M. Garcia, et al., 'A Three-level Framework for LLM-enhanced Explainable AI: From Technical Explanations to Natural Language', *Information Systems Frontiers* (2025).

Bommasani, R., et al., *Foundation Model Transparency Index 2025* (Stanford, CA: Stanford HAI, 2025), https://crfm.stanford.edu/fmti/December-2025/index.html

Brotosaputro, Y., V. Wang and K. Lim, 'AI-Powered Assistive Technologies for Improved Accessibility', *International Transactions on Artificial Intelligence*, 3.1 (2024), https://doi.org/10.33050/italic.v3i1.645

Criado Perez, C., *Invisible Women: Exposing Data Bias in a World Designed for Men* (London: Chatto & Windus, 2019).

Dastin, Jeffery, 'Insight: Amazon Scraps Secret AI Recruiting Tool that Showed Bias against Women', *Reuters*, 11 October 2018, https://www.reuters.com/article/world/insight-amazon-scraps-secret-ai-recruiting-tool-that-showed-bias-against-women-idUSKCN1MK0AG/

'Enhanced Urban Planning for Age-friendly Cities through Disruptive Technologies', *Digital Geography Lab* (University of Helsinki), https://www.helsinki.fi/en/researchgroups/digital-geography-lab/projects/enhanced-urban-planning-for-age-friendly-cities-through-disruptive-technologies

Floridi, L., and M. Taddeo, M. (Eds.), *A Companion to Digital Ethics* (Hoboken, NJ: John Wiley & Sons, 2025).

Greaves, Mark, 'Gender Bias Revealed in AI Tools

Screening for Liver Disease', *UCL News*, 11 July 2022, https://www.ucl.ac.uk/news/2022/jul/gender-bias-revealed-ai-tools-screening-liver-disease

Guo, H., and W. Y. Leong, 'Comparative Review of AI Applications in Urban Transport: Insights from China's City Brain and Singapore's LTA Smart Mobility', *Journal of Innovation and Technology*, 1.7 (2025).

Hossain, S., and S. I. Ahmed, 'Towards a New Participatory Approach for Designing Artificial Intelligence and Data-Driven Technologies' (2021), https://arxiv.org/abs/2104.04072

Kamyab, H., T. Khademi, S. Chelliapan, et al., 'The Latest Innovative Avenues for the Utilisation of Artificial Intelligence and Big Data Analytics in Water Resource Management', *Results in Engineering*, 20 (2023), 101566.

Kooli, C., A. Almulhim and R. Alzahrani, 'AI-driven Assistive Technologies in Inclusive Education', *Sustainable Futures*, 10 (2025), 101042, https://doi.org/10.1016/j.sftr.2025.101042

Kuppusamy, S., M. Meivelu, L. Praburaman, M. M. Alam, A. G. Al-Sehemi, and A. K., 'Integrating AI in Food Contaminant Analysis: Enhancing Quality and Environmental Protection', *Journal of Hazardous Materials Advances*, 16 (2024), 100509, https://doi.org/10.1016/j.hazadv.2024.100509

Naffi, N., 'Deepfakes and the Crisis of Knowing', *UNESCO*, 27 October 2025, https://www.unesco.org/en/articles/deepfakes-and-crisis-knowing

Reid, H., 'IKEA Bets on Remote Interior Design as AI Changes Sales Strategy', *Reuters*, 13 June 2023, https://www.reuters.com/technology/ikea-bets-remote-interior-design-ai-changes-sales-strategy-2023-06-13/

Rojan, Z. 'Financial Fraud Detection Based on Machine and Deep Learning: A Review', *Indonesian Journal of Computer Science*, 13.3 (2025), https://doi.org/10.33022/ijcs.v13i3.4059

Russell, S. J., and P. Norvig, *Artificial Intelligence: A Modern Approach*, 3rd ed. (Upper Saddle River, NJ: Pearson, 2010).

Tatman, R., 'Google's Speech Recognition Has a Gender Bias', *Making Noise and Hearing Things*, 12 July 2016, https://makingnoiseandhearingthings.com/2016/07/12/googles-speech-recognition-has-a-gender-bias/

Šekrst, K., J. McHugh and J. Rodriguez Cefalu, 'AI Ethics by Design: Implementing Customizable Guardrails for Responsible AI Development', (2024), https://arxiv.org/abs/2411.14442.

Vaccaro, M., A. Almaatouq, and T. Malone, 'When Combinations of Humans and AI are Useful: A Systematic Review and Meta-analysis', *Nature Human Behaviour*, 8 (2024), 2293–2303, https://doi.org/10.1038/s41562-024-02024-1

Vallance, C., 'Elon Musk's Grok AI appears to Have Made Child Sexual Imagery, Says Charity', *BBC News*, 8 January 2026, https://www.bbc.co.uk/news/articles/cvg1mzlryxeo

Vallor, Shannon, *The AI Mirror: How to Reclaim Our Humanity in an Age of Machine Thinking* (Oxford: Oxford University Press, 2024).

Vashisht, B., 'AI for Safety: Enhancing Driver Performance and Reducing Accidents with Intelligent Systems', *Journal of Artificial Intelligence and Machine Learning*, 2.3 (2024), 1822–1827, https://doi.org/10.51219/JAIMLD/bhavya-vashisht/404

Vaswani, A., N. Shazeer, N. Parmar, J. Uszkoreit, L. Jones, A. N. Gomez, I. Kaiser, and I. Polosukhin, 'Attention Is All You Need', *Advances in Neural Information Processing Systems*, 30 (2017).

Ventura, A., Starke, C., Righetti, F., Köbis, N., 'Relationships in the Age of AI: A Review on the Opportunities and Risks of Synthetic Relationships to Reduce Loneliness', preprint (August 2025), https://doi.org/10.31234/osf.io/w7nmz_v1

World Economic Forum, *The Future of Jobs Report 2025* (Geneva: WEF, 2025), https://www.weforum.org/publications/the-future-of-jobs-report-2025/

9. Artificial Intelligence, Accessibility and Inclusion

Luigi D'Alonzo and Giuliano Pozza

Inclusion and Accessibility

The process of including people with disabilities, while still presenting lights and shadows, has reached a remarkable maturity in most Western countries and progress has been made in other areas of the world as well. In fact, in many countries people with disabilities participate in schools, services, universities, workplaces and politics. In Italy, for example, the doors to inclusion began to open in the 1970s, and over the past fifty years and more, they have swung wide open, enabling people with diverse support needs to access the opportunities that modern society offers. Increasingly, socio-political decision-making is guided by four paradigms.

First, the importance of an inclusive community environment: people with disabilities are recognised as full members of society who should live and participate within their social communities.

Second, the centrality of relationships: like everyone else, people with disabilities need opportunities for social interaction and belonging. with others and to interact socially. Meaningful interpersonal relationships are essential to feeling part of a group.

Third, the value of responding to personal differences: rehabilitation, social and educational programs must be tailored to the individual needs of each person. The experiences of recent years tell us that we need to abandon the idea of pre-packaged programs based on disability or its severity. Instead, support should align with the individual's personal, social and family context to create a meaningful life plan.

 https://doi.org/10.11647/OBP.0530.09

Fourth, and finally, self-determination is recognised: in recent years, there has been growing awareness that decisions should not be made without the effective involvement of the person with disabilities.

Moreover, the importance of recognising the value of accessibility as the basis of the inclusive process stands out very clearly in Article 9 of the UN Convention of 2006:

> To enable persons with disabilities to live independently and participate fully in all aspects of life, States Parties shall take appropriate measures to ensure to persons with disabilities access, on an equal basis with others, to the physical environment, to transportation, to information and communications, including information and communications technologies and systems, and to other facilities and services open or provided to the public, both in urban and in rural areas. These measures, which shall include the identification and elimination of obstacles and barriers to accessibility.[1]

It is widely accepted that, for a proper inclusive vision of society, the concept of accessibility must be understood as the elimination of all forms of barriers that prevent the independence and participation of persons with disabilities. This leads to an extension of the concept of accessibility, which is not intended exclusively as a protective and categorical norm, limited to forms of disadvantage, but as a universal right of access, through the elimination of barriers and intrinsic limitations to freedom, autonomy and quality of life, with fair and free access to quality services for all.

Artificial Intelligence or Accessible Intelligence?

The term artificial intelligence (AI) is strongly misleading. Philosophers and psychologists have explained in so diverse ways that there is nothing intelligent about AI. Or at least nothing resembling a 'human-like' intelligence. Luciano Floridi is very strong on this point: AI is a matter of 'agency', not intelligence.[2] This is probably true. Other authors,

---

1 United Nations, *Convention on the Rights of Persons with Disabilities and the Optional Protocol Thereto*, adopted 13 December 2006, opened for signature 30 March 2007, in force 3 May 2008, UN Doc. A/RES/61/106, https://www.ohchr.org/en/instruments-mechanisms/instruments/optional-protocol-convention-rights-persons-disabilities

2 Luciano Floridi, *The Ethics of Artificial Intelligence: Principles, Challenges, and Opportunities* (Oxford: Oxford University Press, 2023).

like Y. N. Harari, differentiate between intelligence and consciousness: intelligence is the ability to solve problems, while consciousness is the ability to feel emotions. AI can obtain the former but not the latter. Probably true again, but we must be wary of definitions of intelligence and consciousness: we could not convene on a common one for either so far. On the other hand, Turing would probably say: 'As long as AI is indistinguishable from humans and can solve problems, does it matter?'. Following Turing's chain of thought, we turn to a contemporary benchmark that operationalises this idea. In what follows, we examine the Massive Multi-discipline Multimodal (MMMU)[3] test for generative AI. We focus our attention on this particular implementation of AI for two reasons. First, we believe that many of our conclusions will hold true for AI in general and, secondly, generative AI has a special relevance for inclusion and accessibility. The results of the MMMU test are as follows:

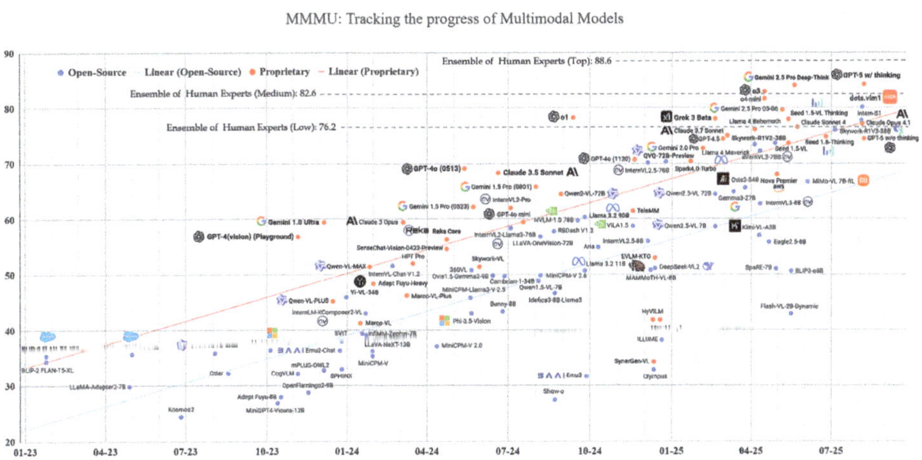

Fig. 9.1 Results from the Massive Multi-discipline Multimodal Test (Xiang Yue et al., 'MMMU', https://mmmu-benchmark.github.io/).

3 Xiang Yue et al., 'MMMU: A Massive Multi-discipline Multimodal Understanding and Reasoning Benchmark for Expert AGI', in *Proceedings of the IEEE/CVF Conference on Computer Vision and Pattern Recognition (CVPR)* (n.p., 2024), pp. 9556–9567, https://openaccess.thecvf.com/content/CVPR2024/papers/Yue_MMMU_A_Massive_Multi-discipline_Multimodal_Understanding_and_Reasoning_Benchmark_for_CVPR_2024_paper.pdf See also https://github.com/MMMU-Benchmark/MMMU

As you can see, many generative AI solutions are already at the level of an 'ensemble of human experts (medium)' in the measured performance. Do not be fooled by the word 'medium' here: the key word is 'ensemble'. It means that the top generative AI models (which are still in their infancy) cover at a medium level of expertise all the domains of the test (art and design, business, science, health and medicine, humanities and social sciences, tech and engineering)! No match for us average humans: it is almost impossible for a single human to be a medium-level expert in all six of these domains. For more details about how the tests are designed, refer to the MMMU website mentioned above.

Besides making available to (almost) everybody the expertise equivalent to that of top-level experts, there is another characteristic of generative AI which is extremely relevant for us: its tremendous capability of handling inputs and outputs in tens or hundreds of different formats and content structures. Multimodal AI tools are already here, but they are still in their adolescence. Their plateau of productivity is expected to arrive in 2-5 years, according to Gartner.[4]

These two facts have significant implications for accessibility and inclusion. Accessibility (a pre-requisite for inclusion) is often a matter of removing barriers by using multiple input and output formats and organising the structure of the content in a way that fits the user's needs. AI solves much of this problem: we can ask our models to prepare content with a tone of voice, a description level and a language that fits the specific audience. Moreover, the same content can be provided as a text, a video, a PDF file, a mind map, a presentation, a podcast... just name it!

The other problem is that sometimes, even if accessibility is formally guaranteed, we can still produce exclusionary or discriminatory outcomes. For example, maintaining a primary website alongside a simplified, reduced-content version for users with special needs does not constitute inclusion; it amounts to segregation.

With AI, the situation is different. Because, regardless of the format or the organisation of the content (which can be personalised based on the needs of the single user), the underlying knowledge base remains the same for everyone. And the intelligence of the knowledge base is, as

---

4 Haritha Khandabattu and Birgi Tamersoy, 'Hype Cycle for Artificial Intelligence, 2025', *Gartner*, 11 June 2025, https://www.gartner.com/en/documents/6579402

outlined above, comparable to that of an ensemble of mid-level human experts, and is rapidly approaching higher levels of expertise.

Now, this is the scenario ahead of us (but partially already here): top-level human experts available to share their knowledge in 1,000 different representations and willing to repeat their explanations 1,000 times if necessary in 1,000 different formats (and multi-language, by the way). This level of accessibility of knowledge is unprecedented in the history of humankind because, believe it or not, it is an intrinsic characteristic of the AI artifacts we are building and not something we have to plan, design and build out of our commitment to the cause. It is just in the DNA, so to speak, of generative AI. Moreover, it is worthwhile to note, that this is a giant step forward not only for people with disabilities but for everyone. This has tremendous potential for true inclusivity, together with some drawbacks that we will explore later in this chapter.

The last point regarding AI and accessibility is that AI is used widely in assistive technologies to boost the performance of almost any digital tool: from speech to text/text to speech to visual recognition to real time captioning, as shown in many studies.[5] And accessibility testing benefits greatly from AI as well.

It is hopefully clearer now why we dubbed AI 'Accessible Intelligence' in our section heading above. In turn, as we presently explore, AI turns personalised learning into a more sustainable option.

AI for Didactic Differentiation

Personalised learning has been a dream for many educators. Unfortunately, most of the time it has been an unreachable dream, since it is hardly sustainable with the limited resources of the school system in many countries. At the core of the idea of personalised learning, there is the widespread awareness that people are different and that they must be respected for their uniqueness, taking into account their particular and indeed special needs. In many countries there is an increasingly widespread presence in schools of students who, in their uniqueness, have problems, peculiarities and specific fragilities, but also

5 See https://www.digitallearninginstitute.com/blog/revolutionising-accessibility:-the-role-of-ai-in-assistive-technology

have remarkable potential. The widespread proliferation in all contexts of certifications attesting to conditions of disability or special needs has also led to the development of the concept of neurodiversity, the idea that neurological and cognitive differences between human beings should not be seen as disabilities or anomalies to be corrected, but as natural variations of the human mind. In other words, neurodiversity celebrates neurological diversity as a form of pluralism, similar to cultural, ethnic or biological diversity. However, all this has consequences that deserve to be highlighted for their importance: the truly inclusive educational path is differentiated teaching. This is a methodological approach that aims to respond to the diversity of students within a classroom by adapting teaching methods and content to the different needs, learning styles, skills and paces of the students. Differentiation involves not only adapting content but also the structure of activities, assessment and the organisation of school space and time. In this context, the teacher takes on a fundamental role as a designer and mediator of learning processes, creating educational experiences that can be effective for every student, enhancing each student's potential and promoting academic success for all. Differentiated instruction must not be seen as an occasional practice, but as a methodology integrated into everyday school life, a continuous process that adapts to different stages and situations of learning.

Carol Ann Tomlinson, who was the first person in the US to systematise differentiated instruction, urged teachers in one of her articles to 'stop studying the to-do list and start studying your students'.[6] Studying, or getting to know your students in depth, is in fact one of the cornerstones of differentiated instruction, understood as 'a basic methodological approach capable of promoting meaningful learning processes for all students in the classroom, aimed at proposing targeted educational activities designed to meet the needs of individuals in an educational environment where it is customary to approach teaching in different ways'.[7]

More specifically, within the framework of differentiated instruction, there is a pre-assessment phase, i.e., an initial, exploratory phase to be

6 C. A. Tomlinson and Jane Jarvis, 'Teaching Beyond the Book', *Educational Leadership*, 64.1 (2006), 16–21.

7 L. D'Alonzo, *La differenziazione didattica per l'inclusione* (Trento: Erickson, 2016), p. 47.

carried out in the classroom and with the class, since it is essential to start with the levels of knowledge and skills already possessed by the students in order to plan activities optimally.

It goes without saying that all activities designed and prepared by the teacher must be planned based on the information gathered during this pre-assessment phase, as it is possible to differentiate on the three levels of content, process and products. First of all, it is essential to differentiate the content that the student is required to learn; secondly, it is very important to differentiate the process that the teacher prepares to encourage students to construct their own knowledge; and finally, it is possible to differentiate the expected final product.

The model of educational differentiation is based mainly on the real knowledge that the teacher must acquire about their students, as differentiation is only possible if the characteristics, strengths and weaknesses of each student are known. In this sense, in the proposal for educational differentiation, the teacher has the opportunity to form flexible and heterogeneous groups based on the readiness levels, interests and learning profiles of the students, i.e., all those elements that need to be gathered and explored in order to tailor teaching to the real needs of the individuals that make up the class group.

Although differentiated instruction cannot be reduced to a pre-established set of strategies, over the years and with the accumulation of concrete experience in schools of all types and levels, both Tomlinson in the American context and the Center for Studies and Research on Disability and Marginality in the Italian context, have developed a series of practical recommendations to support teachers who wish to implement differentiated instruction.[8]

As anticipated, AI can make didactic differentiation a sustainable option. Notwithstanding the fact that human educators are and will be invaluable (and hopefully irreplaceable) actors of differentiated education, AI can help:

- Producing learner-tailored content, thanks to the ability to manipulate concepts and express the same content in different versions.
- Helping to define the best process for addressing the students'

8 *CeDisMa – Centro Studi sulla Disabilità e Marginalità*, https://www.cedisma.it/

needs. AI can guide teachers in finding the right strategies for the student or group of students, a kind of 'teaching tutor' facilitating the navigation of a growing knowledge base.

- Formatting the final product in a way that is more accessible for the intended learner.

We foresee, in the coming years, a flowering of new initiatives in differentiated or personalised learning environments. This will be a tremendous contribution to inclusion strategies.

Is There a Dark Side?

So far, we explored the 'lightness' of AI for accessibility and inclusion, without mentioning any 'weight'. Is it realistic? Unfortunately (or luckily, Kundera would probably say) no. First of all, the fact that AI tools enable greater accessibility does not mean they are accessible themselves.[9] For example, it is common to find accessibility issues in websites created by AI.[10]

Moreover, accessibility is part of a wider context called DEIA, which stands for Diversity, Equity, Inclusion and Accessibility.[11] We will not explore here the Diversity and Equity part of the acronym (on this, see Chapter 8 in this volume), but it is worth remembering that accessibility is a necessary but not sufficient condition for the real goal: inclusion. And, even when our tools are accessible, it is a long journey to foster inclusiveness. An example of an accessible but not inclusive situation is when you have technically accessible technologies that are not available to everyone. This is the case for many AI tools, which are widening (due to high access costs) the digital divide, or AI divide. A minority of the world population can afford top of the class AI technologies. And the

9 Peng Wang, Mengzhen Zhao and Lulu Cheng, 'Artificial Intelligence and Accessibility', in *The Palgrave Encyclopedia of Disability*, ed. by G. Bennett and E. Goodall (Cham: Springer, 2025), pp. 1–6, https://doi.org/10.1007/978-3-031-40858-8_466-1

10 Katelyn Leedy, Makenzie Preston, Jinjuan Feng and Jeba Rezwana, 'Accessibility in the Age of Generative AI Web Based Builders: Evaluating Web Design Tools for Inclusive Practices', in *Proceedings of the 28th International Academic Mindtrek Conference (Mindtrek '25)* (New York: Association for Computing Machinery, 2025), pp. 304–14, https://doi.org/10.1145/3757980.3757989

11 DEI became DEIA in 2021.

divide is widening. The problem is complex and builds on pre-existing issues: access to (high speed) internet, availability of basic technologies, access to AI tools and affordability of such tools. AI is costly and in the current implementations hardly sustainable. With these premises, we can see that AI cannot be for all as it should be. And this is not a problem limited to low-income countries, since the barrier to inclusion can be based on the skills gap. A large part of the population, even in the countries that are leading the AI race, has a sub-optimal access to AI. As UNESCO highlights in a recent report, 'we need to bridge the AI literacy gap'.[12]

Conclusions: Why Inclusion Is Generative

The long history of recognising the rights of people with disabilities in society and the experiences now widespread throughout the world offer us indisputable evidence: when we welcome a person with disabilities, when we respect and offer dignity to those with problems, we inevitably grow as people and as citizens. The presence of persons with a disabilities, with their physical, mental or sensorial limitations, forces the social context to become aware of the duties that every man and woman has towards others. In a welcoming social environment, this attitude becomes a genuine generative element, forcing the social group to develop valuable responses that can positively promote the civil life of all and progress on a cultural, civil, ethical and moral level. Breaking down architectural barriers, building suitable ramps, spacious elevators, sliding doors and safe, obstacle-free roads and paths for people with physical disabilities means building a better world for everyone, even for those without specific needs, even for the young woman pushing her baby in a stroller, even for the elderly person who finds it increasingly difficult to climb stairs or overcome obstacles. The same holds true for digital architectures. Designing a physical ecosystem that is accessible to everyone, for example, including those with sensory impairments, means promoting services dedicated to citizens that can be used by everyone: the acoustic signal at traffic lights that indicates when the light is green

12 Susan Gonzales, 'AI Literacy and the New Digital Divide—A Global Call for Action', *UNESCO* (6 August 2024), https://www.unesco.org/ethics-ai/en/articles/ai-literacy-and-new-digital-divide-global-call-action

for the blind is not only useful for those with visual impairments, but for everyone; tactile paving on roads or sidewalks that allow these people to move around public places independently without assistance are important for every citizen, even the youngest; indoor navigation tools (i.e. a kind of 'Google Maps' for navigating inside buildings) can be beneficial to everyone; accessible web applications can be used profitably by the elderly or people with temporary disabilities. This perspective allows us to view people with disabilities not as a burden on society, but as a resource: people with physical, sensory or mental limitations are not a hindrance to a country's social and civil progress, but can represent an energy at its disposal to promote innovation in all fields, from social environment to production industries, from educational settings to cultural context at large. The clarifying framework must be this: do not operate, work or think only for some, but design for everyone, right from the start. Both in the physical and in the digital word. This is the heart of the inclusive approach: a perspective that sees accessibility and inclusion as a generative, not compensatory, element.

AI DISCLAIMER: the authors did not use AI in writing this chapter. However, AI was used for research purposes in collecting supporting evidence.

References

CeDisMa – Centro Studi sulla Disabilità e Marginalità, https://www.cedisma.it/

D'Alonzo, L., *La differenziazione didattica per l'inclusione* (Trento: Erickson, 2016).

Floridi, Luciano, *The Ethics of Artificial Intelligence: Principles, Challenges, and Opportunities* (Oxford: Oxford University Press, 2023).

Gonzales, Susan, 'AI Literacy and the New Digital Divide—A Global Call for Action', *UNESCO* (6 August 2024), https://www.unesco.org/ethics-ai/en/articles/ai-literacy-and-new-digital-divide-global-call-action

Khandabattu, Haritha, and Birgi Tamersoy, 'Hype Cycle for Artificial Intelligence, 2025', *Gartner*, 11 June 2025, https://www.gartner.com/en/documents/6579402

Leedy, Katelyn, Makenzie Preston, Jinjuan Feng and Jeba Rezwana, 'Accessibility in the Age of Generative AI Web Based Builders: Evaluating Web Design Tools for Inclusive Practices', in *Proceedings of the 28th International Academic Mindtrek Conference (Mindtrek '25)* (New York: Association for Computing

Machinery, 2025), pp. 304–14, https://doi.org/10.1145/3757980.3757989

Tomlinson, C. A., and Jane Jarvis, 'Teaching Beyond the Book', *Educational Leadership*, 64.1 (2006), 16–21.

Wang, Peng, Mengzhen Zhao and Lulu Cheng, "Artificial Intelligence and Accessibility", in *The Palgrave Encyclopedia of Disability*, ed. by G. Bennett and E. Goodall (Cham: Springer, 2025), pp. 1–6, https://doi.org/10.1007/978-3-031-40858-8_466-1

United Nations, *Convention on the Rights of Persons with Disabilities and the Optional Protocol Thereto*, adopted 13 December 2006, opened for signature 30 March 2007, in force 3 May 2008, UN Doc. A/RES/61/106, https://www.ohchr.org/en/instruments-mechanisms/instruments/optional-protocol-convention-rights-persons-disabilities

Yue, Xiang, Yuansheng Ni, Kai Zhang, Tianyu Zheng, Ruoqi Liu, Ge Zhang, Samuel Stevens, Dongfu Jiang, Weiming Ren, Yuxuan Sun, Cong Wei, Botao Yu, Ruibin Yuan, Renliang Sun, Ming Yin, Boyuan Zheng, Zhenzhu Yang, Yibo Liu, Wenhao Huang, Huan Sun, Yu Su and Wenhu Chen, 'MMMU: A Massive Multi-discipline Multimodal Understanding and Reasoning Benchmark for Expert AGI', in *Proceedings of the IEEE/CVF Conference on Computer Vision and Pattern Recognition (CVPR)* (n.p., 2024), pp. 9556–9567, https://openaccess.thecvf.com/content/CVPR2024/papers/Yue_MMMU_A_Massive_Multi-discipline_Multimodal_Understanding_and_Reasoning_Benchmark_for_CVPR_2024_paper.pdf

10. Thinking in the Age of Machines: How AI Shapes and Distorts Human Cognition

Claudia Feiner

A few years ago, I took a speed-reading course. I wanted to read faster, to absorb knowledge more efficiently. If there were a way today to upload information directly into the brain, say through a USB connection, I am not sure I would have the strength to resist. The temptation would be enormous. Finally, I would never forget anything again, never miss a detail, and I would have access to 'everything'. Because I have never had a great memory, I developed early workarounds for this shortcoming: digital folders like OneNote or a heavy leather notebook from Argentina. These tools helped me support my thinking without outsourcing it entirely.

Today, I no longer need a speed-reading course. I type my question into ChatGPT, and in a fraction of a second, I get an answer—often, let us be honest, better than I could have written myself.

That raises a deeper question: is intelligence and by that, the ability to pursue complex goals independent of any specific physical medium? Could it be that what matters is not the atoms themselves, but the stable molecular pattern they form?[1] Or is genuine thought bound to biology in a way machines can never replicate?

For centuries, this has been the core of the mind–body problem: the dualism of flesh and soul. From ancient myths to the dreams of gods

1 This idea of so-called 'substrate independence' is pursued, for example, by Tegmark, Kurzweil, and Moravec.

 https://doi.org/10.11647/OBP.0530.10

and machines,[2] to Turing and beyond, many of the old answers remain not only relevant but strikingly current.

Even in ancient Greece, people tried to imagine the origin of thought. Today we would likely describe the giant Talos from myth as a robot, and Daedalus as a skilled creator of beings that were made, not born.

The term 'artificial intelligence', however, was coined by technology pioneers in the mid-1950s, when machine intelligence was still entirely theoretical. Joseph Weizenbaum created ELIZA and later became a fierce critic of AI.[3] Hubert Dreyfus warned, against strong opposition, that machines would never simulate human understanding because they lacked embodiment.[4] Hans Moravec claimed the opposite: that we are creating cognitive children who will one day surpass us.[5] Roger Penrose insisted that human thought contains something beyond algorithms and perhaps even beyond the physical.[6]

I believe those thoughts are as urgent today as ever. We live in an age where these old but visionary ideas are becoming real: the age of large language models, a world of inevitable cognitive duality between humans and machines.

This ongoing collaboration has already begun to reshape the architecture of our minds, even if we do not notice when we're co-thinking with AI. So the real question is: what kind of thinkers do we become when thinking becomes a joint effort between mind and machine?

In the 1950s, British mathematician and computing pioneer Alan Turing wrote: 'A man would be given away at once by slowness and inaccuracy in arithmetic'.[7] He meant that this is how we would always recognise the human in a Turing Test. That sentence has become reality.

The defining question today is no longer whether artificial intelligence

---

2 Adrienne Mayor, *Gods and Robots: Myths, Machines and Ancient Dreams of Technology* (Princeton, NJ: Princeton University Press, 2018).

3 Joseph Weizenbaum, *Die Macht der Computer und die Ohnmacht der Vernunft* (Frankfurt: Suhrkamp, 1978).

4 Hubert L. Dreyfuss, *What Computers Can't Do: The Limits of Artificial Intelligence* (New York: Harper & Row, 1979).

5 Hans Moravec, *Mind Children: The Future of Robot and Human Intelligence* (Cambridge, MA: Harvard University Press, 1988).

6 Roger Penrose, *Computerdenken* (Heidelberg: Spektrum der Wissenschaft, 1991).

7 Alan Turing, *Computing Machinery and Intelligence* (Oxford: Oxford University Press, 1950).

is smarter than we are. In many cognitive domains, it already is. The question now is: what happens to us when we build systems that no longer feel like tools, but like intellectual rivals?

AI Systems Amplify Our Cognitive Strengths and Sharpen the Mind

Does AI really help us sharpen our minds and enhance our cognitive abilities? We certainly produce astonishing results with its help and when used well, it can significantly boost our output. For instance, I have created entire knowledge bases on various topics by feeding texts into AI systems. This allows me to engage in a kind of personal dialogue with the authors and their ideas. It is as if they're sitting across from me, and I can ask for their advice.

Used this way, AI feels like a strong tailwind. It amplifies our cognitive potential. I feel as though I have access to the knowledge of all humankind, but shaped into answers tailored precisely to my needs. Not only that; I have begun training personalised GPTs to serve as sparring partners on any topic. With them, I can challenge my own logic, ask for counterarguments to a thesis, or explore blind spots in my thinking.

Generative AI also helps us push beyond the natural limits of, let us say, brainstorming. By prompting the system for ideas or concepts, we engage in divergent thinking on a large scale—thinking in many directions at once. As humans, we are left with the task of convergent thinking: filtering, selecting, and evaluating the best options based on our context, goals and values.[8]

In theory, AI enables us to tap into interdisciplinary synergies like never before. Put simply, I can apply insights from one field to a completely different domain, even if I am not familiar with it (yet). If I build an AI-based knowledge pool, I can approach problems like a recipe: a bit of this, a pinch of that. This opens the door to entirely new solutions and encourages fresh, multifaceted perspectives.

And yet, as a society, we face a challenge: on the one hand, we interact with AI as if it were a black box. In fact, many people accept its

8 Zenson Tran, *Know Thy Second Brain: The Art of Collaborating with AI and Yourself* (Self-published print-on-demand, 2025).

results as if by stunning magic. What else should we call it, when there's an instant answer for nearly every question in the world? It is what Arthur C. Clarke described in his Third Law: 'Any sufficiently advanced technology is indistinguishable from magic'.[9]

On the other hand, the actual workings of generative AI and neural networks remain a mystery to most. Few understand how 'the AI' does what it does. What we do see is this: a fleeting thought becomes a structured prompt, and that prompt becomes a fully formed text. We write faster, see clearer, think broader. What is not to like?

AI Shifts the Structure of Thinking Itself

The more mental work we shift from our own minds into AI tools, the more our internal thinking is gradually replaced by external processing. Once the computer begins to think along with us, we begin to think more shallowly.

A study published by MIT in June 2025 showed exactly that. Researchers examined how using AI for writing affected brain activity and memory among fifty-four students. The participants were divided into three groups: those using AI, those using traditional search engines, and those working without any digital aids. The results were clear: students with AI were faster and more efficient—but they also made more reasoning errors.[10] How is that possible?

AI changes the structure of thinking itself. To understand this shift better, it helps to look at the functional anatomy of this erosion.

First, our memory becomes less 'sticky' because we no longer wrestle mentally with the material. Our attention fragments, because answers arrive instantly. And metacognition—the ability to reflect on our own thinking—declines. Why? At least in some contexts, the convenience of AI means we spend less time questioning our assumptions, spotting gaps in reasoning, or verifying the internal logic of an argument. After all, the AI already delivers something that sounds like a good answer.

---

9 Arthur C. Clarke, *Profiles of the Future: An Inquiry into the Limits of the Possible* (New York: Harper & Row, 1973).

10 Nataliya Kosmyna, Eugene Hauptmann, Ye Tong Yuan, Jessica Situ, Xian-Hao Liao, Ashly Vivian Beresnitzky, Iris Braunstein and Pattie Maes, 'Your Brain on ChatGPT: Accumulation of Cognitive Debt when Using an AI Assistant for Essay Writing Task', *arXiv* (2025), https://arxiv.org/pdf/2506.08872

We may produce more and faster, but we may also be thinking less deeply in the process.

This shift from internal to external processing is known as cognitive offloading.[11] When we outsource generative tasks like writing or content creation, it has long-term consequences for our mental faculties. While we may be freeing up cognitive resources, we also become lazier in a metacognitive sense. In practice, that means we slowly lose core capabilities like memory retention, analytical thinking and problem-solving skills. We now know that higher-order functions like planning or critical thinking, which includes things like error monitoring and plausibility checking, also show steady decline when offloaded.[12] And with knowledge always at our fingertips, we run into another problem: we start to confuse information access with understanding. More on that in the next section.

So what now? There is reason for hope. The MIT study also uncovered something encouraging: students who first tried to solve a task on their own, and only then used AI to refine or improve their results, showed significantly higher brain activity. That included spikes in the alpha, beta and theta frequency bands.[13] In other words: the sequence in which we use AI matters. If we first think for ourselves, and only then bring in technological help, we preserve more of our cognitive integrity.

Simply put: thinking and prompting often work best as a sequence, even if, in practice, they both quickly start to intertwine.

At a Cultural Level, the Meaning of 'Knowing' is Being Redefined

If knowledge is always one prompt away, access starts to feel like ownership. Even back in the 1970s, Joseph Weizenbaum stated that 'there is nothing that humans know which cannot, in principle, be made

11 Michael Gerlich, 'AI Tools in Society: Impacts on Cognitive Offloading and the Future of Critical Thinking', *Societies*, 15.6 (2024), https://doi.org/10.3390/soc15010006

12 Sarah Baldeo, *100 Ways to Future-Proof Your Brain in the Age of AI* (Toronto: Arc and Edge Books, 2025).

13 David Sehyeon Baek, 'A Critical Look at MIT's "Your Brain on ChatGPT" and the Accumulation of Cognitive Debt: AI as a Cognitive Tool, Not a Crutch', *LinkedIn* (2025), https://www.linkedin.com/pulse/critical-look-mits-your-brain-chatgpt-accumulation-cognitive-baek-q4mzc/

accessible to computers in some form'.[14] Nearly fifty years after that statement was made, we can safely assume that virtually every word ever written by humans has found its way into the training data of generative AI. And since the launch of the iPhone in 2007, smartphones and herewith access to information has become easier, faster and more affordable than ever before. The access to a vast portion of humanity's accumulated knowledge fits in our palm.

On a cultural level, this has shifted the very meaning of 'knowing'—from embodied understanding to fast, interface-based access.

The generation of digital natives is primarily learning how to retrieve information, but no longer stores it 'internally'. We are experiencing what researchers call digital amnesia.[15] You may know the feeling: we often forget the actual content of a file, but we still remember roughly where we saved it or what to search for in order to find it again.

But being able to retrieve something is not the same as truly understanding it. When we are no longer emotionally involved in the creative process of producing an idea, authorship itself becomes something of an illusion. What does that mean in practice? Here is an example: when people simply copy and paste AI results, they miss out on the emotional experience of wrestling with words or trying to express a thought precisely. When the interface replaces the internal, lived process in which facts are integrated with experience, emotion and values, we gain convenience but we risk losing judgment.

If there is no 'neural friction', no struggle to form a thought, then the final result often lacks what we might call a 'birth pain'. No wonder so many AI-generated texts and images feel interchangeable and emotionally flat. They were emotionally flat from the start.

Another danger is more subtle: if all knowledge feels only one prompt away, mere access can start to feel like 'understanding'. But real knowledge does not arise from retrieving information. It emerges from engaging with it, questioning it, struggling with it.

A 2025 study calls this the 'Comfort-Growth Paradox'. Put simply,

---

14 Joseph Weizenbaum, *Die Macht der Computer und die Ohnmacht der Vernunft* (Frankfurt: Suhrkamp, 1978).

15 Barbara Oakley, Michael Johnston, Ken-Zen Chen, Eulho Jung and Terrence Sejnowski, 'The Memory Paradox: Why Our Brains Need Knowledge in an Age of AI', *SSRN*, 11 May 2025, https://papers.ssrn.com/sol3/Delivery.cfm/5250447.pdf?abstractid=5250447&mirid=1

comfort leads to stagnation. The researchers emphasise that genuine learning and personal growth happen when we face cognitive challenges and experience dissonance, particularly in exchange with others.[16]

Personally, I benefit greatly from outsourcing arithmetic tasks, external memory storage, and especially the ability to search indexed knowledge in the blink of an eye. But for everything else, we would all do well to make an effort—so that our cognitive abilities do not wither, but grow. 'Use it or lose it'. This old saying is once again supported by recent studies on neuroplasticity. The principle is simple: areas of the brain that are heavily used remain adaptable and functionally active. Those that are underused tend to atrophy over time.[17]

And because every experience and human encounter literally shapes us, the human brain continues to change throughout life. That is one key difference between us and AI. Once training is complete, the internal parameters of a neural network, like those used in large language models, remain, at least as of today.

What's To Do?

We oscillate between a kind of bewildered awe at the omnipresence and power of new technologies and the great expectations we place on artificial intelligence.

The challenge in the age of intelligent machines is not whether they can think like us, but whether we still have the will to think for ourselves when we no longer have to.

We must learn to preserve friction in our thinking, even when it would be easier not to. We should force ourselves to read texts before letting them be summarised. We can sketch ideas ourselves before asking AI to render them. We need to re-learn to value the weight of thinking, precisely because technology makes it so easy to feel weightless.

16 Giuseppe Riva, 'Digital "We": Human Sociality and Culture in the Era of Social Media and Artificial Intelligence', *American Psychologist*, 80.9 (2025), 1535–1549, https://doi.org/10.1037/amp0001577

17 Peng Liu, Juliane Doehler, Julia U. Henschke, Alicia Northall, Angela Knaf-Serian, Laura C. Loaiza-Carvajal, Eike Budinger, Dietrich S. Schwarzkopf, Oliver Speck, Janelle M. P. Pakan and Esther Kuehn, 'Layer-specific Changes in Sensory Cortex Across the Lifespan in Mice and Humans', *Nature Neuroscience*, 28 (2025), 1978–1989, https://doi.org/10.1038/s41593-025-02013-1

If we lose that will, we will not be enslaved by AI or robots. We will have surrendered willingly to a convenient kind of immaturity.

Weizenbaum once offered a simple piece of guidance, in the spirit of the old saying: 'Choose your words wisely'. For Weizenbaum, the difference between deciding and choosing was essential. Machines decide based on probabilities and algorithms. Humans choose based on values, moral reasoning, and the burden of consequences.[18]

As human beings, we still have a choice—above all, the choice of who we want to be.

AI DISCLAIMER: the author used AI to translate the original (German) text into English and reviewed the final output personally.

References

Baek, David Sehyeon, 'A Critical Look at MIT's "Your Brain on ChatGPT" and the Accumulation of Cognitive Debt: AI as a Cognitive Tool, Not a Crutch', *LinkedIn* (2025), https://www.linkedin.com/pulse/critical-look-mits-your-brain-chatgpt-accumulation-cognitive-baek-q4mzc/

Baldeo, Sarah, *100 Ways To Future-Proof Your Brain In The Age Of AI* (Toronto: Arc and Edge Books, 2025).

Clarke, Arthur C., *Profiles of the Future: An Inquiry into the Limits of the Possible* (New York: Harper & Row, 1973).

Dreyfuss, Hubert L., *What Computers Can't Do: The Limits of Artificial Intelligence* (New York: Harper & Row, 1979).

Gerlich, Michael, 'AI Tools in Society: Impacts on Cognitive Offloading and the Future of Critical Thinking', *Societies*, 15.6 (2024), https://doi.org/10.3390/soc15010006

Kosmyna, Nataliya, Eugene Hauptmann, Ye Tong Yuan, Jessica Situ, Xian-Hao Liao, Ashly Vivian Beresnitzky, Iris Braunstein and Pattie Maes, 'Your Brain on ChatGPT: Accumulation of Cognitive Debt when Using an AI Assistant for Essay Writing Task', *arXiv* (2025), https://arxiv.org/pdf/2506.08872

Liu, Peng, Juliane Doehler, Julia U. Henschke, Alicia Northall, Angela Knaf-Serian, Laura C. Loaiza-Carvajal, Eike Budinger, Dietrich S. Schwarzkopf, Oliver Speck, Janelle M. P. Pakan and Esther Kuehn, 'Layer-specific Changes

18 Joseph Weizenbaum, *Die Macht der Computer und die Ohnmacht der Vernunft* (Frankfurt: Suhrkamp, 1978).

in Sensory Cortex Across the Lifespan in Mice and Humans', *Nature Neuroscience*, 28 (2025), 1978–1989, https://doi.org/10.1038/s41593-025-02013-1

Mayor, Adrienne, *Gods and Robots: Myths, Machines and Ancient Dreams of Technology* (Princeton, NJ: Princeton University Press, 2018).

Moravec, Hans, *Mind Children: The Future of Robot and Human Intelligence* (Cambridge, MA: Harvard University Press, 1988).

Oakley, Barbara, Michael Johnston, Ken-Zen Chen, Eulho Jung and Terrence Sejnowski, 'The Memory Paradox: Why Our Brains Need Knowledge in an Age of AI', *SSRN*, 11 May 2025, https://papers.ssrn.com/sol3/Delivery.cfm/5250447.pdf?abstractid=5250447&mirid=1

Penrose, Roger, *Computerdenken* (Heidelberg: Spektrum der Wissenschaft, 1991).

Riva, Giuseppe, Digital "We": Human Sociality and Culture in the Era of Social Media and Artificial Intelligence', *American Psychologist*, 80.9 (2025), 1535–1549, https://doi.org/10.1037/amp0001577

Tegmark, Max, *Life 3.0: Being Human In The Age Of Artificial Intelligence* (New York: Penguin Random House, 2017).

Tran, Zenson, *Know Thy Second Brain: The Art of Collaborating with AI and Yourself* (Self-published print-on-demand, 2025).

Turing, Alan, *Computing Machinery and Intelligence* (Oxford: Oxford University Press, 1950).

Weizenbaum, Joseph, *Die Macht der Computer und die Ohnmacht der Vernunft* (Frankfurt: Suhrkamp, 1978).

11. Inclusive and Sustainable AI Maturity Models: How We Can Make a Difference

Giuliano Pozza

Why a Maturity Model

I do not know a single organisation, both on supply and demand side, which is not working on AI, but many, if not most, are struggling with a lack of vision and direction on AI implementation; this often translates into fragmented AI initiatives, typically consisting of pilot projects, proof of concepts, and heterogeneous vertical applications, that most probably will lead to failure and wasted resources. A 2025 MIT Report[1] suggests that, despite huge investments into generative AI, ranging from estimates of $30 to $40 billion, 95% of organisations see no returns. The fragile equilibrium among solid architectures, strong integration with processes, diffuse digital culture (and if necessary, upskilling), risk management, sound governance models and ethical/sustainability considerations is seldom a reality. In many cases, we do not know where we are (in absolute terms or in comparison with other organisations) and we feel that we need support to trace an organic and sustainable path towards our strategic goals. If your organisation is in a similar situation, consider the option of adopting an AI maturity model. A maturity model is a structured framework used to assess an

1 Aditya Challapally, Chris Pease, Ramesh Raskar and Pradyumna Chari, *The GenAI Divide: State of AI in Business 2025* (Project NANDA, 2025), https://mlq.ai/media/quarterly_decks/v0.1_State_of_AI_in_Business_2025_Report.pdf

 https://doi.org/10.11647/OBP.0530.11

organisation's current capabilities, processes or technologies against a set of benchmarks, providing a roadmap for improvement. Of course, selecting the right maturity model (a more descriptive, prescriptive or comparative[2] one) is important and should be aligned with the overall goals of the organisation. A good way to align execution with strategy is to define a Strategic Agenda, linked to the organisation's purpose, as described in Chapter 4 in this volume. The inspiration comes from Michael Porter's Value Based Health Care[3] framework, where all kinds of measurement are used (PROMS, PREMS, Outcome, etc.), but the Strategic Agenda is the lighthouse that ensures the alignment between Vision, Mission, Goals, Objectives and Key Results, to use a common framework derived from the OKR model.[4]

The second reason why maturity models are important is that they stimulate a growing and diffused maturity among all the organisations using them. This is what happened with the Software Engineering Institute's (SEI) Capability Maturity Model (CMM),[5] developed for the software industry, and, in the healthcare sector, with the adoption of the Electronic Medical Record Adoption Model (EMRAM) by the Healthcare Information and Management Systems Society:[6] not only did the top-ranking hospitals (in the USA and worldwide) benefit from the maturity model, but in regions where adoption was widespread and systematic, the entire healthcare ecosystem saw a general rise of the maturity of hospitals overall. And this is relevant for AI too because, as Harari pointed out in his latest book,[7] *Nexus*, the impacts of poorly implemented AI resemble environmental pollution: mitigating the harm requires coordinated effort from all actors involved. Sometimes, just one actor managing risk poorly or introducing unethical and unsustainable

---

2 R. B. Sadiq, N. Safie, A. H. Abd Rahman and S. Goudarzi, 'Artificial Intelligence Maturity Model: A Systematic Literature Review', *PeerJ Computer Science*, 7 (2021), e661, https://doi.org/10.7717/peerj-cs.661

3 Michael E. Porter, 'What Is Value in Health Care?', *New England Journal of Medicine*, 363.26 (2010), 2477–2481, https://doi.org/10.1056/NEJMp1011024

4 Ryan Panchadsaram, 'What is an OKR? Definition and Examples', *What Matters*, https://www.whatmatters.com/faqs/okr-meaning-definition-example

5 *CMMI Institute*, https://cmmiinstitute.com/

6 *Electronic Medical Record Adoption Model (EMRAM)*, HIMSS Maturity Models (Healthcare Information and Management Systems Society, Inc.), https://www.himss.org/maturity-models/emram

7 Y. N. Harari, *Nexus* (London: Fern Press, 2025).

practices can jeopardise everyone's efforts. Moreover, companies working with AI also have a social responsibility: developing socially sustainable AI platforms is fundamental to prevent humans from being crushed by AI and digital technologies. Some of the guiding principles for a healthy relationship between humans and AI are highlighted by Prof. G. Riva in his intriguing article 'Digital We: Human Sociality and Culture in the Era of Social Media and Artificial Intelligence'.[8] Many of these good practices could be fruitfully embedded in AI maturity models to make them more socially sustainable.

What Maturity Model

First, we need to clarify that the following is not a systematic literature review of the AI maturity models landscape. Several such reviews have been published,[9] but these are either narrow in focus or have become obsolete. From our analysis, a few models emerge. We will discuss them briefly, leaving it to the reader to explore them (and not only them, because there is a wide and growing set of models out there) thoroughly following the links in the references:

- SEI AI maturity model:[10] the SEI approach starts from the assumption that AI is a form of software and therefore draws on its rich culture of software-development maturity models. There are five levels (Exploratory AI, Implemented AI, Aligned AI, Scaled AI and Future Ready AI). The goal of the model is not only certification or pure benchmarking, but the creation of an actionable roadmap. At the time of writing, the details of the model are not publicly available.
- MIT CIRS maturity model:[11] the MIT maturity model is built

8 Giuseppe Riva, 'Digital "We": Human Sociality and Culture in the Era of Social Media and Artificial Intelligence', *American Psychologist*, 80.9 (2025), 1535–1549, https://doi.org/10.1037/amp0001577

9 Sadiq, Safie, Abd Rahman and Goudarzi, 'Artificial Intelligence'.

10 I. Ozkaya et al., 'A Preliminary Report on a Model for Maturing AI Adoption: From Hype to Achieving Repeatable, Predictable Outcomes', *Software Engineering Institute*, December 2025, https://doi.org/10.1184/R1/30840476

11 Peter Weill, Stephanie L. Woerner and Ina M. Sebastian, 'Building Enterprise AI Maturity', *MIT Center for Information Systems Research Research Briefing*, 14 (2024), https://cisr.mit.edu/publication/2024_1201_EnterpriseAIMaturityModel_

around four stages: Experiment and Prepare, Build Pilots and Capabilities, Develop AI Ways of Working, Become AI Future Ready. At the time of writing, only 7% of the companies evaluated by MIT are at stage 4. The details of the model are not publicly available.

- Accenture-Stanford maturity model:[12] this model is also built around four stages (Principles, Program, Practice, Pioneer) and is specifically targeted at implementing responsible AI. It covers both sides of the AI coin: risk mitigation and value creation. What is noteworthy is that it explicitly encompasses inclusion, diversity and sustainability themes.
- Gartner maturity model:[13] the stages of this model are Planning, Experimenting, Stabilisation, Scaling and Leading and the capabilities analysed are AI Strategy, AI Value, AI Organisation, AI People and Culture, AI Governance, AI Engineering and AI Data. The model is accessible only to Gartner's clients, so we will not explain it further. It is worth mentioning because it has been used as a basis for other models.
- Microsoft maturity model:[14] Microsoft, as Accenture, is explicitly focused on responsible AI. The stages are Latent, Emerging, Developing, Realising, Leading. The material is publicly available. On the responsibility side, there is a stronger focus on accountability, transparency, risk management, privacy and security (called 'RAI practices' in the model), more than on sustainability and inclusion.

WeillWoernerSebastian

12 'Thrive with Responsible AI: How Embedding Trust Can Unlock Value', *Accenture*, November 2024, https://www.accenture.com/us-en/insights/data-ai/rai-from-risk-to-value

13 'AI Maturity Model & Roadmap Toolkit', *Gartner* (Chief Information Officer Research), https://www.gartner.com/en/chief-information-officer/research/ai-maturity-model-toolkit

14 Mihaela Vorvoreanu, Amy Heger, Samir Passi, Shipi Dhanorkar, Zoe Kahn and Ruotong Wang, 'Responsible AI Maturity Model', *Microsoft Research Technical Report*, MSR-TR-2023-26, May 2023, https://www.microsoft.com/en-us/research/publication/responsible-ai-maturity-model/

- Jisc maturity model:[15] the Jisc model is focused on the higher education sector and brings together ideas from a number of other more general AI maturity models, including ones from Microsoft and Gartner. The five stages are Approaching and understanding, Experimenting and exploring, Operational, Embedded, Transformational.

This list must not be considered as complete or exhaustive. We are aware, for example, that many AI solution providers have developed their own maturity models, but here we included only one vendor model, because we found it particularly relevant to our context (for its focus on inclusion and sustainability) and because it is one of the foundations of the Jisc model. As the Special Interest Group of EUNIS for Inclusive and Sustainable AI[16] (SIG AI4ALL for brevity), we remain open to considering additional maturity models in the future or developing of our own.

Conclusions: When and How

Maturity models are, in our view, a powerful way to endorse inclusive and sustainable practices in AI implementation. We also do believe that having clarity about purpose and strategic goals is paramount for getting the best out of a maturity model, whatever our choice.

While there are, for example, digital sustainability maturity models,[17] we think that incorporating sustainability and inclusion in general AI maturity models could bring more benefits. For this reason, the SIG AI4ALL is interested in keeping dialogue open with all the actors developing AI maturity models. As a follow-up to the present work, AI4ALL will study the importance of maturity models for inclusion and sustainability in AI.

We are aware that what we shared so far is not conclusive and should be viewed more as a starting point than a final work. However,

15 Michael Webb, 'A Maturity Model for AI in Tertiary Education', *Artificial Intelligence (National Centre for AI)*, 26 September 2022, https://nationalcentreforai.jiscinvolve.org/wp/2022/09/26/a-maturity-model-for-ai-in-tertiary-education/

16 'Inclusion & Sustainability in AI (AI4ALL)', *EUNIS Task Forces (European University Information Systems Organisation)*, https://eunis.org/task-forces/ai4all/

17 T. Abdulghani, N. Abdelkafi, H.-R. Lange and H. Winkler, 'Paving the Green Path: A Maturity Model for Digital Decarbonization', *Procedia CIRP*, 130 (2024), 1020–1027, https://doi.org/10.1016/j.procir.2024.10.201

we liked the idea of ending the book looking ahead to an open path, something to work on in the next phase of our journey. Currently, SIG AI4ALL is exploring the aforementioned maturity models, and we are ready to offer our contribution to review/validate the models based on DEIA (Diversity, Equity, Inclusion and Accessibility) and sustainability aspects. We hope maturity models could help balance lightness and weight in AI development and dissemination, therefore we will promote the design and use of inclusive and sustainable AI maturity models.

AI DISCLAIMER: the author did not use AI in writing this chapter. However, AI was used for research purposes in collecting supporting evidence.

References

Abdulghani, T., N. Abdelkafi, H.-R. Lange and H. Winkler, 'Paving the Green Path: A Maturity Model for Digital Decarbonization', *Procedia CIRP*, 130 (2024), 1020–1027, https://doi.org/10.1016/j.procir.2024.10.201

'AI Maturity Model & Roadmap Toolkit', *Gartner* (Chief Information Officer Research), https://www.gartner.com/en/chief-information-officer/research/ai-maturity-model-toolkit

Challapally, Aditya, Chris Pease, Ramesh Raskar and Pradyumna Chari, *The GenAI Divide: State of AI in Business 2025* (Project NANDA, 2025), https://mlq.ai/media/quarterly_decks/v0.1_State_of_AI_in_Business_2025_Report.pdf

CMMI Institute, https://cmmiinstitute.com/

Electronic Medical Record Adoption Model (EMRAM), HIMSS Maturity Models (Healthcare Information and Management Systems Society, Inc.), https://www.himss.org/maturity-models/emram

Harari, Y. N., *Nexus* (London: Fern Press, 2025).

'Inclusion & Sustainability in AI (AI4ALL)', *EUNIS Task Forces* (*European University Information Systems Organisation*), https://eunis.org/task-forces/ai4all/

Ozkaya, I., 'A Preliminary Report on a Model for Maturing AI Adoption: From Hype to Achieving Repeatable, Predictable Outcomes', *Software Engineering Institute*, December 2025, https://doi.org/10.1184/R1/30840476

Panchadsaram, Ryan, 'What Is an OKR? Definition and Examples', *What Matters*, https://www.whatmatters.com/faqs/okr-meaning-definition-example

Porter, Michael E, 'What Is Value in Health Care?', *New England Journal of Medicine*, 363.26 (2010), 2477–2481, https://doi.org/10.1056/NEJMp1011024

Riva, G., 'Digital "We": Human Sociality and Culture in the Era of Social Media and Artificial Intelligence', *American Psychologist*, 80.9 (2025), 1535–1549, https://doi.org/10.1037/amp0001577

Sadiq, R. B., N. Safie, A. H. Abd Rahman and S. Goudarzi, 'Artificial Intelligence Maturity Model: A Systematic Literature Review', *PeerJ Computer Science*, 7 (2021), e661, https://doi.org/10.7717/peerj-cs.661

'Thrive with Responsible AI: How Embedding Trust Can Unlock Value', *Accenture*, November 2024, https://www.accenture.com/us-en/insights/data-ai/rai-from-risk-to-value

Vorvoreanu, Mihaela, Amy Heger, Samir Passi, Shipi Dhanorkar, Zoe Kahn and Ruotong Wang, 'Responsible AI Maturity Model', *Microsoft Research Technical Report*, MSR-TR-2023-26, May 2023, https://www.microsoft.com/en-us/research/publication/responsible-ai-maturity-model/

Webb, Michael, 'A Maturity Model for AI in Tertiary Education', *Artificial Intelligence (National Centre for AI)*, 26 September 2022, https://nationalcentreforai.jiscinvolve.org/wp/2022/09/26/a-maturity-model-for-ai-in-tertiary-education/

Weill, Peter, Stephanie L. Woerner and Ina M. Sebastian, 'Building Enterprise AI Maturity', *MIT Center for Information Systems Research Research Briefing*, 14 (2024), https://cisr.mit.edu/publication/2024_1201_EnterpriseAIMaturityModel_WeillWoernerSebastian

Post Scriptum: The AI4ALL Special Interest Group Explained

Giuliano Pozza

Artificial intelligence is the hype of the moment, yet two critical issues remain underrepresented in mainstream discussions: sustainability and inclusion. We face an unacceptable (or unbearable) risk of developing AI tools that serve only a privileged segment of the global population, driven by unsustainable costs and environmental impacts, as well as services that are neither accessible nor inclusive. This digital divide could lead to consequences far worse than those we have already encountered.

To address these challenges, the EUNIS Inclusion and Sustainability in Artificial Intelligence (AI4ALL) Special Interest Group (SIG) was established in 2024, to explore and explain the deep connections between inclusion, sustainability and the future of AI; to spread awareness about the need for an 'AI for All' that focuses on inclusion and sustainability challenges; and to encourage private and public organisations to consider inclusion and sustainability in their AI development, regulations and use.

The vision of AI4ALL is to promote an inclusive and sustainable AI journey. Only by considering AI, sustainability and inclusion together we can avoid the risk of developing 'elite technologies' that will increase the digital divide and increase the risk of misuse.

The goals of the EUNIS SIG on AI4ALL therefore are:

1. Creating a cross-initiative community that fosters the dissemination of information and best practices among EUNIS members and relevant stakeholders in the public sector and academia.

 https://doi.org/10.11647/OBP.0530.12

2. Enabling inclusion and sustainability to become key factors in AI development, AI regulations and AI use.
3. Sharing knowledge and best practices, aiming for better understanding and a future state of AI operations where inclusion and sustainability are the norm.
4. Promoting and stimulating projects and initiatives that aim to support and improve inclusion and sustainability in AI operations.
5. Exploring university strategies, requirements and responsibilities towards engagement with AI, while securing inclusion and sustainability criteria.
6. Undertaking risk assessment on current AI developments with regard to inclusion and sustainability, in higher education and research.

This book specifically stems from goal n. 3 of the SIG (sharing knowledge), while the AI maturity model initiative launched in the 'Bonus Track' is closely related to goal n. 4 (promoting and stimulating projects).

For further information or to join the group, please send an email to one of the SIG co-leaders: Giuliano Pozza (giuliano.pozza@eunis.org), Bonaria Biancu (bonaria.biancu@eunis.org) or John Magnus Furseth Kallevik (john.m.kallevik@eunis.org).

AI DISCLAIMER: the author did not use AI in writing this chapter.

Contributors

Luigi D'Alonzo is a full Professor of Special Education in the Faculty of Education at the Università Cattolica del Sacro Cuore, Rector's Delegate for Inclusion, and the Director of the Center for Studies and Research on Disability and Marginality (CeDisMa). He is also the former editor of the scientific journal 'Italian Journal of Special Education for Inclusion' and a Past President of SiPeS (Italian Society of Special Education). He is the Director of the Master's Degrees in 'Teaching and Psychopedagogy For Students With Autism Spectrum Disorder', 'Teaching And Psychopedagogy For Students With Attention Deficit/Hyperactivity Disorder (Adhd-Ddai)' and 'Augmentative And Alternative Communication (Aac)', and the Director of the Specialization Course for Support Teachers and National Coordinator of Directors of Specialization Courses for Support Teachers. He has been a member of the Technical Secretariat for Research Policies of the MIUR (Ministry of Education, Universities and Research), the Ministerial Technical-Scientific Committee of the Permanent Observatory for the Integration of Students with Disabilities and the Ministerial Technical-Scientific Committee on SLDs (Specific Learning Disorders). He is the author of many scientific publications aimed at teachers, educators, and researchers.

Claudia Feiner is a Senior Data Consultant at DEGES. She fosters the strategic use of data and AI to build digital twins and therefore to power smarter and more resilient infrastructure across Germany's federal transport network. She is a seasoned tech strategist with over twenty years of experience across global enterprises. Her career includes leadership roles in the automotive sector and consulting. At Porsche, she covered Esports, Metaverse and Web3, long before they became mainstream. At Diconium, she advanced future-oriented topics like

AI for German OEMS. Having spent her career at the intersection of industry, IT, software and infrastructure, she brings an unusual depth of insight into industrial and digital worlds. She connects IT, engineering and executive leadership. Along the way, she has become a strong voice for diversity and inclusion and is widely regarded as a thought leader in various fields. She's been celebrated as one of Germany's 40 Over 40 (2022), Top 100 Heads (2021) and a top LGBT+ voice. As an ambassador, speaker and author, she raises awareness for her topics through articles, podcasts and editorial contributions across various platforms.

Laura Maria Ferri is Associate Professor of Management at the Università Cattolica del Sacro Cuore. Within the same university, she collaborates with ALTIS Graduate School of Sustainable Management, an international research and education centre for the study and promotion of a responsible and competitive business culture, where she is Senior Lecturer and Leader of the 'Custom and Granted Research' Team. She teaches in graduate and undergraduate courses and does scientific research on topics related to business management sustainability and innovation. She is also Scientific (co-)Director of the Executive Master's in Innovability Management, the first of its kind, aimed at developing managerial knowledge and competences on the integration of digital innovation and sustainability.

John D. Halamka M.D., M.S., is an American business executive and physician. He is president of the Mayo Clinic Platform, a group of digital and long-distance healthcare initiatives. Trained in emergency medicine and medical informatics, Halamka has been developing and implementing healthcare information strategy and policy for more than twenty-five years. He specialises in artificial intelligence, the adoption of electronic health records and the secure sharing of healthcare data for care coordination, population health, and quality improvement. In 2020, Halamka was elected to the National Academy of Medicine (NAM). Prior to his appointment at Mayo Clinic, he was chief information officer at Beth Israel Deaconess Medical Center. He is a practicing emergency medicine physician. As the International Healthcare Innovation Professor at Harvard Medical School, Halamka helped the George W. Bush administration, the Obama administration and governments around the world plan their healthcare information strategies.

Cal Innes is a leading voice in digital sustainability in the UK, working at the intersection of technology, environmental responsibility and ethical AI. As a Digital Sustainability Specialist supporting UK education and research, he helps institutions across the country embed sustainable digital strategies. Cal's expertise spans carbon-conscious IT, AI ethics, digital waste reduction, and green digital transformation. Cal chairs the FE and Skills Digital Sustainability Community and edits the widely-read *Digital Sustainability Newsletter*. He has contributed to national policy discussions, helping organisations understand and act on the hidden environmental costs of digital infrastructure.

John Magnus Furseth Kallevik is CTO and systems architect at the University of Stavanger, where he leads digital transformation as Head of the Section for Service Development. With over thirty years of experience bridging software, security and human systems, he works in the space where machines meet people, designing technology that simplifies, supports and connects. His background in music, visual media and cybersecurity informs his ability to translate complex systems into intuitive, engaging services. Kallevik regularly gives talks and workshops across sectors on AI, digital transformation and information security, with a focus on inclusion, sustainability and ethical technology use. He believes public services and education should empower people through technology, not overwhelm them, and that digital systems must remain rooted in human needs and democratic values. Outside of work, he enjoys cycling, kayaking and climbing, and often finds his best ideas while immersed in nature, where observing systems in motion helps inspire new ways to simplify the digital ones.

Anand Padmanabhan is Vice President and Chief Information Officer at Fordham University, New York, where he oversees the university's IT vision, strategy, as well as the university's research computing. As a visionary CIO, Anand brings a rare blend of business acumen, cultural intelligence and values-driven leadership to complex organisations. A published researcher, Anand's current research focuses on gender gaps in STEM, examining how pedagogy influences self-efficacy and persistence among first- and second-year undergraduates. Anand has more than two decades of technology leadership, having served as CIO at five universities, including NYU Stern, as corporate CIO for a $9 billion revenue IT services firm, and as global CTO for a $680 million (series B) education start-up. He advises EdTech start-ups and serves on Microsoft, Zoom and Knack's higher education advisory boards. He has received Top 100 CIO awards in both the United States and India and is listed in New York State's 2025 Who's Who in Emerging Technologies. Anand holds an MBA from NYU Stern School of Business, an MSc in Computer Engineering from Louisiana State University, and a BE from Madras University.

Giuliano Pozza is the Chief Information Officer at Università Cattolica del Sacro Cuore. He is a biomedical engineer, and he has extensive experience in IT strategy, governance, change and program management in complex environments, specialising in higher education, healthcare and pharmaceutical sectors. He acquired certifications in DASSM (Disciplined Agile Senior Scrum Master), ISACA CISM (Certified Information Security Manager) and CGEIT (Certified in the Governance of Enterprise IT). He is also a coach trained according to the ICF (International Coaching Federation) standards. He was the President of the Italian Association of Healthcare Information System Professionals (AISIS). He served as CIO of some of the most important Italian Hospitals and worked for Accenture. He likes hiking and mountaineering in the Alps, running marathons, reading and sometimes writing. He is a EUNIS Ambassador and the co-leader of the AI4ALL EUNIS Special Interest Group.

Evelien Renders is Advisor for Internationalisation of Education at SURF, the Dutch cooperative for IT in education and research. She specialises in interoperability, open standards and IT architecture in higher education, with a focus on cross-border collaboration and learner-centred digital ecosystems. As President of EUNIS, the European network for digital transformation in higher education, and board member of 1EdTech Europe, she advocates for public values, trust and alignment between institutions and technology providers. Evelien co-develops visual tools that make enterprise architecture and interoperability more accessible to diverse stakeholders, supporting systemic change across the sector. Trained as a classicist, she brings a deep interest in how language, art and structure shape our thinking, bridging past and future in the way we design digital education. She thrives in complex, multi-stakeholder environments where values, technology and policy intersect.

Bianca de Teffé Erb is Partner at Deloitte, founder and leader of AI Ethics Practice, focusing on algorithmic governance and ethics, AI risk and regulatory compliance. With over a decade of consulting experience, she has advised public institutions, supranational bodies, and major industrial groups, including NATO, ESA, UN, FAO and ECDC to develop policies and guide responsible AI adoption in compliance to EU AI Act and international standards. She also collaborates with academia and sectorial institutions as an author of ground-breaking research papers driving societal change, such as the report, 'Towards an Ethics by Design Approach for AI', presented to the EU Parliament, and she is an active speaker and thought leader who contributes to international conferences (United Nations, ISPI, AI Festival, etc.). In 2018, she was named one of Forbes Italy's Top 30 Under 30, ranking first in the Enterprise Technology category. She is a sociologist and is currently pursuing a PhD in Artificial Intelligence at the University of Milan, where her research focuses on the impact of the future of work in the public sector.

Simon Whittemore is an experienced senior consultant and educator with a background in strategic innovation and change programmes, skills and learning, digital transformation and organisational development. Passionate about education as a force for good, Simon works with universities as a lecturer, writer and programme manager. A higher education and adult learning specialist, who teaches business strategy and organisational design, he has over twenty-five years' senior experience in public and private sectors working at national and international levels. Formerly Head of Change—Enterprise at Jisc, Deputy Head of Business and Community Policy at HEFCE, and Senior Consultant at Capgemini HQ in Paris, Simon has led national programmes and digital solutions in higher education strategy, policy and funding, as well as developing corporate methods and standards. Simon is the author of a range of papers and articles on Transversal Competencies, Sustainable Employability and Skills-based Workforce Strategies, Digital Innovation and Skills, Learning Cultures, Sustainability and Multiculturalism. He is an oenophile, art aficionado, rugby man and nature lover.

Index

About the Team

Jessica Schwarz, Community Support Officer, EUNIS, was the project manager for this book.

Alessandra Tosi was the managing editor.

Adèle Kreager proof-read this manuscript and compiled the index.

Jeevanjot Kaur Nagpal designed the cover. The cover was produced in InDesign using the Fontin font.

Annie Hine typeset the book in InDesign. The main text font is Tex Gyre Pagella and the heading font is Californian FB.

Jeremy Bowman produced the PDF, paperback, and hardback editions and created the EPUB.

The conversion to the HTML edition was performed with epublius, an open-source software which is freely available on our GitHub page at https://github.com/OpenBookPublishers

Lucy Barnes was in charge of marketing.

This book was peer-reviewed by two anonymous referees. Experts in their field, these readers give their time freely to help ensure the academic rigour of our books. We are grateful for their generous and invaluable contributions.

This book need not end here...

Share

All our books — including the one you have just read — are free to access online so that students, researchers and members of the public who can't afford a printed edition will have access to the same ideas. This title will be accessed online by hundreds of readers each month across the globe: why not share the link so that someone you know is one of them?

This book and additional content is available at https://doi.org/10.11647/OBP.0530

Donate

Open Book Publishers is an award-winning, scholar-led, not-for-profit press making knowledge freely available one book at a time. We don't charge authors to publish with us: instead, our work is supported by our library members and by donations from people who believe that research shouldn't be locked behind paywalls.

Join the effort to free knowledge by supporting us at https://www.openbookpublishers.com/support-us

You may also be interested in:

Artificial Intelligence in Higher Education

A Phenomenological View

Edited by Sencer Yeralan et al.

https://doi.org/10.11647/OBP.0525

Ethics of Socially Disruptive Technologies

An Introduction

Edited by Ibo van de Poel et al.

https://doi.org/10.11647/OBP.0366

Transparent Minds in Science Fiction

An Introduction to Alien, AI and Post-Human Consciousness

Paul Matthews

https://doi.org/10.11647/OBP.0348

www.ingramcontent.com/pod-product-compliance
Ingram Content Group UK Ltd.
Pitfield, Milton Keynes, MK11 3LW, UK
UKHW062006071026
15591UKWH00023B/868

9 781805 11898